"Biographies are, indeed, back. Not only will students read them, biographies provide an easy way to demonstrate particularly important historical themes or ideas. . . . Undergraduate readers will be challenged to think more deeply about what it means to be a woman, citizen, and political actor. . . . I am eager to use this in my undergraduate survey and specialty course."

—JENNIFER THIGPEN,
Washington State University, Pullman

"These books are, above all, fascinating stories that will engage and inspire readers. They offer a glimpse into the lives of key women in history who either defied tradition or who successfully maneuvered in a man's world to make an impact. The stories of these vital contributors to American history deliver just the right formula for instructors looking to provide a more complicated and nuanced view of history."

—ROSANNE LICHATIN,
2005 Gilder Lehrman Preserve
American History Teacher of the Year

"The *Lives of American Women* authors raise all of the big issues I want my classes to confront—and deftly fold their arguments into riveting narratives that maintain students' excitement."

—WOODY HOLTON,
author of *Abigail Adams*

Lives of American Women

Carol Berkin, Series Editor

Westview Press is pleased to launch Lives of American Women. Selected and edited by renowned women's historian Carol Berkin, these brief, affordably priced biographies are designed for use in undergraduate courses. Rather than a comprehensive approach, each biography focuses instead on a particular aspect of a woman's life that is emblematic of her time, or which made her a pivotal figure in the era. The emphasis is on a "good read," featuring accessible writing and compelling narratives, without sacrificing sound scholarship and academic integrity. Primary sources at the end of each biography reveal the subject's perspective in her own words. Study Questions and an Annotated Bibliography support the student reader.

Dolley Madison: The Problem of National Unity by Catherine Allgor

Lillian Gilbreth: Redefining Domesticity by Julie Des Jardins

Alice Paul: Equality for Women by Christine Lunardini

Rebecca Dickinson: Independence for a New England Woman by Marla Miller

Sarah Livingston Jay: Model Republican Woman by Mary-Jo Kline

Betsy Mix Cowles: Bold Reformer by Stacey Robertson

Sally Hemings: Given Her Time by Jon Kukla

Shirley Chisholm: Catalyst for Change by Barbara Winslow

Margaret Sanger: Freedom, Controversy and the Birth Control Movement by Esther Katz

Barbara Egger Lennon: Teacher, Mother, Activist by Tina Brakebill

Anne Hutchinson: A Dissident Woman's Boston by Vivian Bruce Conger

Angela Davis: Radical Icon by Robyn Spencer

Catharine Beecher: The Complexity of Gender in 19th Century America by Cindy Lobel

Julia Lathrop: Social Service and Progressive Government by Miriam Cohen

Mary Pickford: Women, Film and Selling Girlhood by Kathy Feeley

Elizabeth Gurley Flynn: The Making of the Modern Woman by Lara Vapnek

Lillian Gilbreth

Redefining Domesticity

JULIE DES JARDINS

Baruch College

LIVES OF AMERICAN WOMEN
Carol Berkin, Series Editor

WESTVIEW
PRESS
A Member of the Perseus Books Group

Westview Press was founded in 1975 in Boulder, Colorado, by notable publisher and intellectual Fred Praeger. Westview Press continues to publish scholarly titles and high-quality undergraduate-and graduate-level textbooks in core social science disciplines. With books developed, written, and edited with the needs of serious nonfiction readers, professors, and students in mind, Westview Press honors its long history of publishing books that matter.

Published by Westview Press,
A Member of the Perseus Books Group

Find us on the World Wide Web at www.westviewpress.com.
Every effort has been made to secure required permissions for all text, images, maps, and other art reprinted in this volume.

Westview Press books are available at special discounts for bulk purchases in the United States by corporations, institutions, and other organizations. For more information, please contact the Special Markets Department at the Perseus Books Group, 2300 Chestnut Street, Suite 200, Philadelphia, PA 19103, or call (800) 810-4145, ext. 5000, or e-mail special.markets@perseusbooks.com.

Library of Congress Cataloging-in-Publication Data
Des Jardins, Julie.
  Lillian Gilbreth : redefining domesticity / Julie Des Jardins ; foreword by Carol Berkin.
    p. cm. — (Lives of American women)
  Includes bibliographical references and index.
  ISBN 978-0-8133-4763-9 (pbk. : alk. paper) 1. Gilbreth, Lillian Moller, 1878–1972. 2. Women—United States—Biography. 3. Work and family—United States—History. 4. Women industrial engineers—United States—Biography. 5. Family life—United States—Biography. I. Title.
  HQ1413.G527D47 2013
  658.5'4092—dc23
  [B]
                                              2012012514
10 9 8 7 6 5 4 3 2 1

CONTENTS

SERIES EDITOR'S
FOREWORD

In 1948, when *Cheaper By the Dozen* hit the bookstores, millions of Americans came to know Lillian Gilbreth as the doting mother of twelve children. Yet to those who knew the importance of Gilbreth's innovative work, she was not simply "Mother of the Year," she was also "The Mother of Industrial Psychology." In the books and movies made about her family, Lillian appears to be the very model of post–World War II domesticity—a stay-at-home wife and mother, happy to bow to her husband's judgment and to devote herself to raising her family. In reality she was a pioneer in the science of industrial management and psychology, the holder of honorary degrees, an international lecturer, and the recipient of a dozen awards and engineering society medals. Yet Gilbreth's story is not one of unchallenged success. In the early twentieth century, she faced the gender bias common in graduate and professional programs that were not specifically defined as female areas. Her conviction that subjective factors were as important to consider as objective ones was originally rejected by her male colleagues in the newly emerging profession of industrial engineering. And, while her husband Frank lived, the engineering profession viewed her as a helpful assistant to his work rather than as a full and equal partner in the many studies of time and motion the couple produced together. Lillian did not complain about these challenges she faced as a woman. She remained convinced that employers must consider the human needs of workers, and, in time, both political leaders and business managers would agree. During the Depression, she turned her exceptional skills to the task of improving the circumstances in which women labored in the paid work force, and later she focused on the setting in which wives and mothers worked—the kitchen and the home. Gilbreth was often ahead of her time—but she was willing to wait for American society to catch up.

As Julie Des Jardins shows us in this biography, Gilbreth's life story illustrates the opportunities and the barriers facing women who wanted both professional careers and a satisfying family life in the late nineteenth century and in the decades before the modern feminist movement. Gilbreth was, as Des Jardins notes, a pioneer, not simply in her path-breaking studies of factory efficiency or in her creative redesign of the center of domestic life, the kitchen, but also in her remarkable efforts to balance work and family and to demonstrate that there was no contradiction in being both a woman and an engineer, a mother and an individual with a satisfying career.

In examining and narrating the lives of women both famous and obscure, Westview's Lives of American Women series populates our national past more fully and more richly. Each story told is not simply the story of an individual but of the era in which she lived, the events in which she participated, and the experiences she shared with her contemporaries. Some of these women will be familiar to the reader; others may not appear at all in the history books that focus on the powerful, the brilliant, or the privileged. But each of these women is worth knowing. In their personal odysseys, American history comes alive.

Carol Berkin

AUTHOR'S PREFACE

Cheaper by the Dozen's Mother, Lillian Gilbreth:
A Woman Who Defied All Categories

If younger generations of Americans haven't read the classic book *Cheaper by the Dozen*, perhaps they have heard about the 1950 film adaptation or the late twentieth-century remakes. The original novel, written by a sister and brother, recalled their coming of age in suburban New Jersey in the 1910s. Gathering some of their most vivid memories, they embellished them a bit and offered them up for publication after World War II, when Americans were nostalgic for stories that reinforced traditional family values. The book was so popular that it spawned the film version and a highly anticipated sequel *Belles on Their Toes* two years later. This book, too, was light-hearted fare despite its treatment of a darker chapter in the family's story. Dad, the larger-than-life Frank Gilbreth Sr., had passed away, leaving his wife Lillian Gilbreth in charge of a home, a business, and eleven children.

That there were only eleven living siblings, no longer an even dozen, was a detail left out of the Gilbreths' novel, since it was not conducive to the tone they were trying to strike. But the greatest departure from reality may have been in the depiction of the novel's retiring matriarch, Lillian Gilbreth, who appeared incapable of self-assertiveness, when she appeared at all. Dad ruled the roost in *Cheaper by the Dozen* and featured as the central figure in nearly all the anecdotes his children recalled for postwar readers. "Before her marriage, all Mother's decisions were made by her parents. After her marriage, the decisions were made by Dad," Ernestine and Frank Jr. maintained. "It was Dad who suggested . . . that both of them become efficiency experts." Perhaps more surprisingly, they also claimed that it was Dad's imperative, not Mom's, to have a family of a dozen children.[1]

Aside from her alleged dabbling in efficiency work, the Lillian Gilbreth of *Cheaper by the Dozen* appeared to be the proverbial "Woman Who Lived in a Shoe," overwhelmed by her prodigious offspring had it not been for her rule-making husband. Readers likely conjectured in the literary silence that she tended to domesticity almost exclusively behind the scenes, soothing hurt feelings in the wake of her husband's blustery refusals to let daughters wear provocative swimsuits or attend dances unchaperoned. Her influence, one can only presume, was quiet and unequivocally feminine. She did little to tweak this image after her children's novel came out in 1948. In fact, when asked, she stated that her years married to Frank Gilbreth were the most significant of her life. It was as if she had nothing else to show for herself other than obediently raising his dozen children.

Only at the end of *Cheaper by the Dozen* do readers get the slightest glimpse of the real Lillian Gilbreth's resolve to work outside the home, and it only seems acceptable because her husband is dead and she is desperate to preserve his legacy. Readers are not privy to the fact that, together, she and Frank Gilbreth had run an engineering firm, given scores of professional papers, published eight books and hundreds of articles, conducted courses on industrial management, and maintained a household of servants, schedules, and a dozen children. In fact, Lillian Gilbreth may have been responsible for the lion's share of the work in these joint endeavors. To the outside world, she appeared the helpmeet to a more qualified professional man. But in the Gilbreth household, everyone understood that Mom was an industrial consultant, a credentialed psychologist, an originator of ideas, a writer of texts, a designer of experiments, a supervisor of homework, and a soother of scrapes and hurt feelings all rolled into one.

No book that sought to reinstate traditional family life could ever succeed in revealing Lillian Gilbreth in all of her dimensions, and yet readers of *Cheaper by the Dozen* may find something subversive in this literary portrait, if they care to look. Although her children emphasized their father's patriarchal authority, it was authority subtly influenced by the quieter, more effective control wielded by a mother, who, although not the protagonist of the story, was implicitly a partner of equal standing and the parent with more understanding of emotions and needs. When Dad yelled, Mom cushioned the blow. When he went too far, she was the voice of reason. There is a sense that Lillian Gilbreth let Frank be impudent Frank Gilbreth, but then she quietly cleaned up his messes when he wasn't looking. She was an effective, and perhaps far more efficient, parent and communicator in the end.

If her children had provided glimpses of their mother's life before motherhood, readers would have seen a young woman who went to college to defy traditional marriage, not to embrace it. And while readers of *Belles on Their Toes* saw a widow more independent and savvy than the wife of *Cheaper by the Dozen*, this image still did not do justice to Lillian Gilbreth. Her children's fictional account gave no sense of the extent to which she realized economic autonomy, intellectual fulfillment, and professional success on her own terms and how much she forged paths for other women to do the same. She continued to work more than full time, outside the home, nearly fifty years after Frank Gilbreth's death in 1924. And thus, although nothing was more traditional than marrying and rearing a dozen children, the truth is that Lillian Gilbreth defied every other expectation of well-to-do women coming of age in the late nineteenth and early twentieth centuries. She attended college, earned a doctoral degree, and became an industrial engineer, a professor, a breadwinner, a domestic guru, and a consultant for US presidents. If her own children failed to acknowledge her many hats, it's no wonder that most Americans don't know her name in the twenty-first century.

Actually, there was a time when Lillian Gilbreth held a distinctive, albeit unfixed, place in American popular culture. Men and women on the street once knew her in the 1920s, the '30s, the '40s, the '50s, and even the '60s, even if they weren't always sure what to make of her. The popular press referred to her as "Mother of the Year," (1957) but also as "the greatest woman engineer in the world," (1954) and "The Mother of Industrial Psychology."[2] Magazine editors decided that she belonged on lists of the "Greatest American Women" (1930s), even if they couldn't come to a consensus as to why this was the case.

Lillian Gilbreth was multifaceted, to be sure, and this fact may be the reason that she has since been forgotten; she defies facile categorization, so historians have taken the easier road of neglecting her altogether. By all indications, Lillian seemed to sanction the neglect. She was never adamant about getting her name on books and papers she and Frank Gilbreth coauthored, and she leaves very little autobiographical material behind. Upon her husband's death, she published the story of his life and work, entitled *The Quest of the One Best Way* (1925), which she asked the Society of Industrial Engineers to publish immediately in tribute. Her autobiography, *As I Remember*, she wrote and published privately in 1941, but it was only retrieved and made more widely available to the public in 1998. It is telling that, aside from the title, the story is written in the third person; to say "I" felt too assertive to Lillian Gilbreth, especially when she had spent years saying "Frank this," "Frank that," or sometimes an occasional "we." Like so many women married to prominent men, she had mastered the art of obscuring her work from view.

Luckily, the following rendition of Lillian Gilbreth's life benefits from historians and family members who filled in many of her silences. Jane Lancaster's *Making Time: Lillian Moller Gilbreth—A Life Beyond "Cheaper by the Dozen"* (2004), is the most recent and comprehensive of the biographical works on Gilbreth to date, and thus it is used extensively in this narrative. Laurel Graham's *Managing on Her Own: Dr. Lillian Gilbreth and Women's Work in the Interwar Era* is a thorough account of Gilbreth's professional life and intellectual contributions to industrial management and psychology, while Edna Yost's *Frank and Lillian Gilbreth: Partners for Life* (1949) remains an informative, though dated, source on the Gilbreths' work and life together. Amusing, if not always accurate, versions of Gilbreth family life in the early twentieth century are Ernestine Gilbreth Carey and Frank Gilbreth Jr.'s *Cheaper by the Dozen* (1948) and the sequel *Belles on Their Toes* (1951). Later Frank Jr. went on to write the more reflective *Time Out for Happiness* (1970), which contains insightful commentary on Gilbreth family life.[3]

This book makes no claim to be as comprehensive as most of the books above; if it covered Lillian Gilbreth's life from birth to death, it would be told alongside a backdrop of events spanning nearly a century of modern American history. She lived through an industrial revolution, the passing of women's suffrage, two waves of organized feminism, and two monumental world wars. In terms of shifts in cultural notions of American womanhood, she was born a Victorian, morphed into a "New Woman (1880–1920), and anticipated, to some degree, the "Superwoman" ideal that materialized after the Women's Liberation Movement of the late 1960s and 1970s. Her eyes are windows on too many social, cultural, and economic events to note them all; so much could be broached that is only alluded to in these pages, particularly with regard to the last third of her life. She evokes many conversations, but here most attention is paid to the light she sheds on notions of *domesticity* in American life, primarily in the years of her young womanhood, active motherhood, and early widowhood through the Great Depression of the 1930s. She lived and worked furiously for another forty years, but the Depression serves as a sort of narrative apex in her career, because it supplied the confluence of forces that brought her unique perspective, position, and contributions in American life into clearest view.

Whether historians have emphasized her contributions to industrial processes, homemaking, or changing definitions of womanhood, it is clear that Lillian Gilbreth was a pioneer. Because pioneers tread uncharted terrain by definition, they are never easy to characterize in simple terms. Hers was a path with no blueprints, and thus it is difficult to classify the kinds of science, professionalism, and feminism she espoused, and to discern whether she was a scientist, a professional, or a feminist at all. Rather than label her, it may be more productive to try to understand how she negotiated labels or defied them altogether. She proved that unspoken concepts like "woman engineer," "working mother," "professional wife," or "domestic expert" weren't cultural oxymorons, even when most Americans thought they were. Through Lillian Gilbreth's life, a perspective of shifting work and gender roles in America comes into view.

In the tradition of "great man" history, some biographers have called Lillian Gilbreth the "Mother" of any number of engineering innovations, in addition to her dozen children, much the same way biographers refer to Thomas Edison and Albert Einstein as "Fathers" of their important discoveries. The strategy has worked to garner prestige for Gilbreth in the conventionally historical sense, and yet it has done little to make the private woman better appreciated and understood. Lillian Gilbreth's "greatness" does not lie in lists of her formal accomplishments and official discoveries. The seemingly trivial details of her private, daily, domestic, and routine experience are most meaningful, since they reveal her as typical and extraordinary at once. To tend to these particulars is to acknowledge the value and influence of the private home, much as Lillian Gilbreth did when she applied scientific methods to housewifery. She understood that the balance one struck between public and private, professional and domestic spheres was the key to a fulfilling life, just as it is the key to telling her story in a meaningful way.

The details of her daily routine provide an interesting perspective on the modern concept of "work-family balance." Americans at the turn of the century did not talk about men's work, let alone women's work, in these terms, and yet it is impossible to describe what she was trying to achieve day in and day out without invoking a sense of balance. Her view of balance shifted over time and context, but it was the flexibility of her vision that she successfully propagated through her work and by example. Her efficiency studies in factories and homes saved time, money, and physical energy, but their greater purpose was to allow others—most often women—to strike some sense of balance for themselves. Lillian Gilbreth's story is not a road map for modern women seeking families and careers, but it may just inspire them to be their own guides on paths to self-fulfillment.

Julie Des Jardins

1

Lillie Moller's Victorian World, 1878–1895[1]

In May of 1878, Annie and William Moller of Oakland, California, gave birth to a blue-eyed, redheaded baby and named her Lillie. It would have been a happier occasion if Annie weren't inconsolably worried for herself and her newborn child. Her first daughter Adelaide had died in infancy, and she feared that her new baby girl would fail to thrive like the last. Luckily, her fears proved unwarranted. Although young Lillie was an anxious, antisocial child, she was intellectually curious and physically robust. She went on to live to the age of ninety-four, despite her mother's fears. To Annie's chagrin, her daughter asserted her independence at the age of twenty-one by changing her name to Lillian. This bold gesture seemed appropriate on the eve of her college graduation in a new century— what better way to shirk the dependent femininity her mother embodied? Annie Moller accepted her daughter's independent spirit in time but not before trying, as so many mothers of her upbringing did, to shape her daughter in her mold.

One could hardly blame her for trying, for hers was the only model of womanhood Annie knew; any other seemed, in her eyes, to be failed femininity at best. She was the daughter of wealthy parents, and she had known constant pampering, having never really been charged with the care of another human being until she became a mother herself. Her parents, the Delgers, were of German descent; they raised her in the

Lutheran Church and with all the refinements. She played the piano and harp competently, read the classics aloud, and appreciated high art as if raised in the great museums of Europe. She also was blessed with curly brown tresses and a shapely figure. She was a vision, and her parents knew it: they kept her cloistered at home so as to not court the wrong sort of suitors. Annie was raised to be the quintessential gentlewoman of the Victorian age—refined and always leaving something to be desired.

Although the term "Victorian" refers to the reign of Queen Victoria in England (1837–1901), it is apt here, for it also describes the broader cultural sensibilities in well-to-do classes of Anglophones, including Americans, particularly in regard to gender and sexuality. After the first Industrial Revolution in the early nineteenth century, an ideology of separate spheres rigidly delineated the roles of American men and women: in the ideal world, the former occupied the public realm of business and politics, and the latter, the private realm of the home. Not all American families achieved this ideal of separate spheres, because it required leisure and privilege that working women, rural women, and most women of color did not enjoy. But for women who could afford the luxury of staying home, their cloistered domestic existence conferred a heightened degree of moral authority. This was, in essence, a sort of social power gained through keeping house, rearing children, and staying out of the fray of politics—a form of influence when women had little legal and economic power. Annie Delger had this influence by birthright, and her parents saw to it that it remained untarnished while their daughter remained in their home.

Of course, not all women of privilege conformed to the strict social rules laid before them. Annie had a rebellious older sister named Matilda, for instance, who had secretly eloped in her late teens, thus shirking the protocols of proper courtship and embarrassing her parents. Likewise, Annie's other sister Lillie, after whom Annie named her daughter, later became the subject of gossip when she, too, divorced, remarried, and took on a career. Vowing that their young Annie would never be tempted into the same circumstances, the Delgers acted swiftly when they discovered that their seventeen-year-old was paying special attention to a boy in town. They sent her to finishing school in Germany in 1872, where contact with boys was forbidden, and they vowed that she would never be introduced to any suitor who did not meet their approval beforehand. Their older daughters' ill-fated decisions, as they viewed them, had jeopardized the social standing of the entire family. To make connections in the right circles, Annie's interactions with men had to be carefully controlled.

The Delgers had emigrated from Germany to New York in 1847 and moved to San Francisco three years later. The timing was not accidental. Frederick Delger, like many men, moved west to capitalize on the gold rush of 1849. He proved more successful than most, not because he found gold, but because he shrewdly turned a profit outfitting the miners who looked for it. While Levi Strauss made durable denim trousers for the miners, Delger made his fortune providing them with work boots to match. From there, he invested his money in real estate, buying up acres of land in what would eventually be downtown Oakland. When Frederick Delger died in 1897, he was worth millions. His heirs, Annie's family, lived on a majestic estate that stretched a full city block in the nicest part of town.

Annie lived a sheltered life on the estate with three other siblings—two girls and a lone boy, Eddie. Though all the children received the best education that money could buy, Eddie's schooling diverged from his sisters'. He was never a serious student, but his parents took his intellectual training seriously indeed, even sending him east to Harvard to study law. Annie attended convent schools in Oakland and San Jose before being sent off to the boarding school in Germany. The Delger girls' education didn't include math or science; their lessons featured "cultured English" and the "social arts." Annie Delger was intellectually curious, but she accepted her fate as given: schooling for girls was nothing more than cultivating refinements to become attractive marriage material. Describing her mother's education decades later, Lillian Gilbreth explained that almost no emphasis was placed on her mother's "physical fitness" or "mental alertness." For the Delger girls, their "social adjustment" had the greatest bearing on their future prospects.

German boarding school was supposed to complete Annie's cultivation before finding a suitor for her to marry. On the way to accompanying their daughter overseas, the Delgers took a train to New York and called upon the Mollers, a prominent German family with whom they wanted to be better acquainted. The Mollers were "old money," that is, the family had made its fortune in Germany, and John Moller successfully added to it when he took his family's sugar-refining business to the States. It appealed to the Delgers that the Mollers lived honestly but expensively with their children on several floors of a lavish building on Thirty-Seventh Street in Manhattan. They were just the sort of people with whom they hoped young Annie could ingratiate herself, and they proved eager when an opportunity arose for introductions.

Indeed the Delgers aspired to play by the social rules of the New York elite, and Annie was helping them succeed. Nevertheless, there were many rules to master and pitfalls to avoid. The choosing of marriage partners was a calculated transaction between families of high society. Although it was acceptable for women to marry men they did not know well, parents had to think them proper for purposes of social standing. Young women were supposed to be chaste yet have enough veiled sex appeal for well-bred suitors to pursue them. If and when spouses were incompatible, separation was acceptable, but divorce was not. In the case of the latter, the woman suffered the greater stigma, for a proper lady, many presumed, was supposed to give a man little reason to stray. Women's lack of legal status in marriage perpetuated a paradox: a woman's femininity was defined through her ability to marry and have children, and yet she had little autonomy once she accomplished these ends. Marriage was, in this sense, salvation and sentence at once. Legally, a married woman had little more status than chattel. She was a husband's possession, no longer with possessions of her own. In this circumscribed Victorian world, young women like Annie Delger wanted desperately to marry, but, once they did, they could hope for little more than to find fulfillment by wielding feminine influence on their husbands and their children.

The Mollers would have preferred a more understated family to join with theirs, for privately they thought the Delgers ostentatious and their exploits out West too opportunist to be dignified. But their eldest son, twenty-six-year-old William, a tall and stately heir to the family fortune, was completely enraptured by young Annie Delger when they met during her brief stay in 1872. He wanted to marry her, and his parents politely consented. The couple would marry in Hamburg, they decided, after Annie completed a year of school abroad. The Delgers enthusiastically approved.

Annie and William returned to New York as husband and wife in 1873; shortly afterward, Annie was pregnant. No one was surprised, because babies were expected within the first year of marriage. Few Victorians practiced birth control, and when they did it was typically simple abstinence. Privately, women had ideas about when their bodies were likely to conceive children, though they were not always correct. Even when they were, few women felt emboldened to reject a husband's sexual advances when they believed pregnancy would result, for cultural, let alone legal, notions of marital rape did not yet exist. And hence, whether Annie was prepared for motherhood or not, within the year she bore Adelaide, the baby who died amid the summer heat in 1874. The climate and the loss of the child caused her health to deteriorate further, and William worried for his wife. He followed doctors' orders, sold his share of the sugar business, and moved his wife back to the milder climate of California just before Lillie was born.

From this point forward, Annie's physical fragility became a recurring leitmotif in the Moller household. William pampered her with a staff of servants and rarely let her do things alone; she remained in a perpetual state of convalescence for the rest of her married life. Although William's parents were devastated to see them leave New York, the Delgers were delighted to have their daughter living within walking distance of her childhood home. On the West Coast, Annie could take better advantage of the alternative medicine practiced in Chinatown, for she believed that it was the key to making her stronger to bear more children. Indeed she spent exorbitant amounts of her husband's money on herbs, leaves, and other medicines intended to alleviate her migraines and exhaustion. Li Po Tai, a doctor known by the San Francisco elite, regularly provided licorice and other roots for Annie's "womb problems," and apparently the measures worked. In the next two decades she conceived and bore five more girls in two-year intervals, followed by three boys in the same orderly fashion.

If Annie was a "hypochondriac," she was no more so than other women she knew in the 1870s. She came of age when proper women were seen—and saw themselves—as too delicate to engage in physical labor or intellectual pursuits. Back East in Massachusetts and New York, some women of her age and social standing were attending college in the Seven Sister schools—Vassar, Wellesley, Bryn Mawr, Smith, Radcliffe, Barnard, and Mount Holyoke—which began to open their doors to the daughters of privileged families after the Civil War. But by no means was the "college" education they received designed to prepare them for the paid professions after graduation. Medical experts supported the belief that women engaged in physical activity, formal education, and paid work were at grave risk to their reproductive health. Harvard medical professor Edward Hammond Clarke, most notably, wrote a popular treatise on the subject in 1873 called *Sex in Education*, which supported a conclusion that middle-class Americans already believed: college learning was too taxing on women's bodies to be useful to them. Because rigorous study tapped women of the reserves they needed to make babies, he determined, it must be severely limited or curtailed altogether.[2]

Most middle-class Americans also agreed that a college education was unnecessary, given the calling of proper women to raise their children at home. They needed enough education to make children moral citizens but not enough to be able to earn income or participate in political and intellectual life. Of course, poorer women, the ones, for instance, employed by the Moller and Delger families, were forced to work for a wage as domestic servants or industrial workers, but they, too, risked their physical and moral well-being, the experts believed, because the home was the place where true women cultivated feminine virtue and conserved their energy for reproduction. The fact that working women left the home, in other words, was the reason for their depravity; some privileged members of the industrial elite were downright sanctimonious on this point, urging women who worked for a wage to return home and find religion as a way of bettering their economic circumstances. Lillian Gilbreth's parents belonged to this elite social class, exalting their delicate women as the moral guardians of society. Afforded the luxury of not working outside the home, their women presumably hadn't been sullied by the corruption of politics or the business dealings of men in the public sphere. William Moller perceived his wife as just this kind of woman: her physical weakness was proof of her moral force.

As a child, Lillie became accustomed to preparing her mother's medical elixirs during her perpetual states of bed rest. Mother appeared to be a fragile figure, but in point of fact there is no telling of the extent to which her ailments were clinically real. Victorian women frequently complained of weakness and illness, and gentlemen were raised to treat their wives as delicate hothouse flowers, always in need of special care. In a society in which women had little command over their sexual lives, feigning illness may have been a quiet and effective way to quash the sexual advances that led to unwanted pregnancy. But illness was also a mental preoccupation in lieu of more fulfilling endeavors outside the home. Annie had domestic obligations—the decorating of rooms, the managing of domestics, and the organizing of social engagements—but as a rich woman with a household of servants, one wonders if she subconsciously yearned for more to do.

Although Annie was a woman supposedly tapped of vigor, she was able to nurse her nine children successfully, when all was said and done. Lillie, the eldest, had nursed the longest, as Annie hadn't the heart to force her weaning. Baby Lillie slept on a cot in her parents' room so that her anxious mother could feed her on demand—at least until Lillie the toddler finally weaned herself. Annie became pregnant just six weeks later, with the girl known affectionately as Gertie. During every pregnancy that followed William continued to tend to Annie with kid gloves. "Why do you act this way Papa?" Lillie asked him. "So that Mama won't be ill," he replied. His wife's demise seemed always on his mind.

When Annie wasn't pregnant, William reluctantly permitted her to take herself off to the shops in downtown San Francisco, but he paced the floors awaiting her safe return. He "did not realize," reflected Lillian Gilbreth in 1941, "that his small daughter interpreted this as fear that she'd never come back."[3] Looking back on these anxious moments, when Papa fretted and the maids speculated in whispers about their mistress's failing health, Lillian Gilbreth believed that this worry exhibited by other people contributed to her being a pathologically anxious child. She often stood vigil over her mother when she slept or watched at the gate outside the house on afternoons when Mama was due back from tea at her grandparents' estate. Indeed Lillie's childhood was filled with warm familial bonds, but it was also self-professedly dominated by fear—fear that she would lose her mother, which turned into a fear of doctors, a fear of men, and a fear of being drawn out of her insulated shell. Much of her energy in girlhood was devoted to keeping the outside world from creeping in, keeping all who were not family at arm's length, and clinging desperately to things most familiar. Like so many privileged Victorian girls, she had been raised to think that influences outside the home had potential to harm and corrupt.

By six, Lillie was too terrified of social interaction to be put in school with children her age, and thus Annie kept her home long after other girls had been sent off for "finishing." Paradoxically, this insular existence may have been a source of Lillian's self-assurance later in life: Annie educated her daughter thoroughly, as a professional teacher would, but she nurtured, rather than intimidated, keeping her sensitive daughter's self-confidence intact. She made spelling lists and flash cards and gave Lillie daily assignments after breakfast. To Grandfather Delger's dismay, William and Annie did not speak German at home, and thus Lillie learned their native tongue from books. Annie thought it just as well. Her daughter did love books.

From the moment she could read, books had been Lillie's refuge—starting with Mother Goose, the Brothers Grimm, and Hans Christian Anderson and then moving on to the Alcott novels, Dickens, Dumas, and eventually Kipling and Thackeray. For now, Lillie felt more comfortable in the company of literary characters than that of real people, and she loved to immerse herself in their worlds. There were surprisingly few books that she wouldn't read. She devoured the sentimental novels that belonged to her mother in which predictably the heroines managed to succumb to conventions of marriage and motherhood by the end. But there were her father's adventure stories too, classics such as *The Three Musketeers* and *The Count of Monte Cristo*, which also fascinated her. The heroes were invariably male, but Lillie often wondered what it felt like to have their physical courage and live on their unconventional terms.

Later, in her teens, Lillie began to appreciate the special breed of heroine in the works of British novelist George Eliot (Marian Evans), perhaps because these women showed wit and strength while rejecting conventional femininity. There was the smart, socially conscious Dorothea Brooke in *Middlemarch*, for instance, a wealthy woman who was more interested in designing better cottages for her uncle's mistreated tenants than in designing a lavish wardrobe for parties. Annie Moller thought some of the books Lillie read were inappropriate, as they did little to resign her daughter to the dependent domesticity she sought for her in womanhood. But she indulged her daughter's literary preferences anyway. Books calmed the nerves and stimulated the mind of a girl who strangely resisted the social world of her peers. For now, they refined young Lillie better than anything else.

The Mollers hoped that their efforts to improve their daughter's confidence at home would eventually embolden her at school. For a time it appeared that music might be the vehicle to draw her out. Her most treasured family ritual was to gather around the piano to sing her favorite songs. Papa played "Way Down upon the Swanee River," and Mama played a mix of Beethoven, Handel, waltzes, and polkas for the children. Eventually, as Lillie became an accomplished pianist in her own right, she played the accompaniments. The greatest challenge as she became more skilled, however, was performing for audiences that consisted of more than just the Mollers, the Delgers, or her cousins, the Browns. For a long time she dreaded the concerts in which her piano teacher expected her to perform. Nothing frustrated the Mollers more than having a daughter who was uncomfortable in social situations. She was painfully shy—not a fortunate trait, given the marriage market her parents knew awaited her. They held out hope that one day Lillie would come into her own.

Forcing the issue too soon, Annie enrolled her daughter in the private Snell's Seminary when she turned eight years old, only to regret it. The experience of reciting in front of so many children proved traumatic, and Lillie ran home at lunchtime, begging to never have to return to school. Annie reluctantly agreed to wait longer for her daughter to be ready to forge relationships with children her age. When Lillie turned nine, Annie tried yet another experiment, enrolling her daughter in public school with children who were younger and hopefully less intimidating. The experiment worked, and, after much adjustment, Lillie transitioned into a classroom with children her age. But even then it was clear that she was unpopular with her peers. Every Valentine's Day her mother tried to conceal her own handwriting on cards that she addressed to her daughter and quietly sent to school, so that it looked as if they had come from others. Lillie wasn't fooled; typically the only valentines she received were ones boys sent her in jest.

The teachers could see that Lillie's problems were not academic but social: she preferred their company to that of other children, and she seemed downright petrified of boys. No doubt, typical schoolyard teasing had an effect on her sense of self-worth; Lillie considered herself inept and unattractive, a girl who would never interest boys, so why try? Annie, too, worried that her eldest daughter was destined to be a spinster. In her day, Annie had been known as a compelling conversationalist, and her talent in the social arts had always given her, she felt, an advantage over quieter, less refined girls like her daughter. She decided that she had to intervene more actively in ameliorating Lillie's social deficiencies, and she went to great lengths to make her appear confident and poised in front of others. There were gymnastics and calisthenics classes to make Lillie more self-composed and dance school to improve her general deportment. Meanwhile, she learned to sew and take care of her siblings, all in preparation for the inevitable day, Annie hoped, when Lillie would have a full house of her own.

Indeed Lillie took great comfort in home life and showed proclivities for the domestic arts. She found little need for companionship at school, as her cousins, the Browns, came over regularly and her siblings took up so much of her time. Taking charge of the Moller family rituals was hardly a chore because they gave Lillie such comfort; in fact, many of them she re-established in her own home with Frank Gilbreth decades later. Her parents threw birthday dinners for each of the children, which remained private affairs despite the common practice among the Oakland elite of throwing coming-out parties lavish enough to make the local society pages. Lillie's more intimate birthday celebrations suited her just fine; every May she looked forward to receiving her special cake and the books she itemized on her birthday list. Every November she insisted on preparing the same extensive Thanksgiving menu, and every December she made it her task, as the eldest girl, to manage the wrapping of presents and the trimming of the Christmas tree. Father read out the names on the packages and waited until all else had been opened before pulling out the "New York Box" from Grandma and Grandpa Moller, who sent their grandchildren the latest in Manhattan fashions. The rituals continued through New Year's Eve, as Lillie organized the return of ornaments back to their boxes and father made a bonfire of the tree.

One year Lillie received, along with her Christmas presents, a little golden pin, a small token of appreciation her parents wanted her to have for managing the house while they were out East with the Mollers. Regardless of its monetary value, the pin was priceless in Lillie's eyes. She sobbed when she opened the box and saw it, for it proved that even as the family grew larger, she was honored for her place within it. Mama and Papa made every child in the Moller household feel special in his or her own way. William hated when any child was missing from the dinner table and asked after each of them until he knew their whereabouts. Annie had a way of making each one think that his or her homemade gifts were the best that she ever received. If she ever were to have children, Lillie vowed that she would give them the same love, encouragement, and individual attention. In a big family, it was imperative that all members felt cherished and unique.

The familial bonds forged in the Moller house slowly gave their eldest daughter the confidence and sense of security she needed to interact with the outside world. It was a great relief when Lillie showed signs of excitement about entering Oakland Public High School in the fall of 1892. Oddly it was the same school that her contemporaries the literary lights Jack London and Gertrude Stein found boring and stifling and couldn't wait to leave. For fourteen-year-old Lillie, however, it provided the sense of belonging that she had never felt before. Still awkward around her peers, she started to express herself in her writing, especially in poetry, which she contributed to the school magazine to rave reviews. For the first time she felt the gratification of peer acceptance; it was enough to propel her further out of her shell, even to write the poem selected for the graduating class.

Most influential to Lillie was an English teacher named Elsie Lee Turner, an enthusiastic pedagogue who encouraged her to explore her literary interests. Turner was, to any observer, the epitome of respectability: her dress was meticulously neat, and she exuded a feminine charm. But what Lillie so admired was that Turner did not fear being perceived as intellectual; she read her books, taught them to others, and made a respectable living with her literary knowledge. Lillie decided that she was the exact mold of what a quiet, studious girl could become, despite her mother's fears that appearing too bookish was unfeminine in the eyes of future suitors.

Although many school districts throughout the country continued to mandate that married women leave the teaching profession, presumably to serve as teachers to their own children at home, Turner was an early exception to the rule, teaching well after she married and had a family. Lillie viewed her as living proof that studious young girls did not necessarily turn into unattractive and unhappy old maids. Motherhood and career did not have to be mutually exclusive paths. In Lillie's late Victorian world, Turner was exceptional, but she was not all that unusual in society at large. By the 1890s, when Lillie was in high school, other young women in San Francisco had liberated themselves from domestic duties to work, reform, and socialize with men and other women in the public sphere. They were by no means typical, but they were certainly not alone.

Lillie had the model of Elsie Lee Turner to emulate, but she lived too cloistered an existence to get a full sense of the changing sensibilities in the air. Her family remained tight knit—"clannish," as she described it. And, just as she was taking more interest in activities at school, the pressure to stay home intensified—Mother was still in the throes of having babies. In fact, Annie's three youngest children, her first and only sons, arrived in Lillie's teen years. Their births had been desperately hoped for, and the Mollers were both elated and relieved when all three boys were born without incident. With little men to raise, William moved his family into a larger seven-bedroom mansion on Prospect Avenue. The change of house brought a seismic shift in the family's expectations of Lillie as the eldest female sibling. Annie took sole charge of her eldest son and assigned the youngest girls to Gertie and Lillie, virtually to raise on their own. The cribs of the youngest girls were put in the eldest girls' room so that they could be tended to in the middle of the night, much as Annie had done when Lillie was an infant. When Billy Jr. was born in 1895, Lillie, now a high school junior, took him on too, soothing him to sleep at all hours of the night.

And thus, just as her schoolmates' worlds were expanding, Lillie's was becoming more and more relegated to the Moller estate. She felt pangs of guilt when she stole away to study or peruse the library bookshelves; it was implicitly understood that when she was not in school, she was to take babies off her mother's hands. Annie never dissuaded Lillie from feeling this way, and she made it clear that domesticity was the destiny of a well-to-do woman. It was Mama's duty to manage all dealings "within the gate," she told her eldest; it was Papa's to manage everything else outside it. Men excelled in industry and business, she explained, and women in housework and childcare. To ask boys and girls to traverse these boundaries was to defy the natural order of things. The Moller boys thus rarely performed household tasks that were not "mechanic" in nature, and, with so many females in the house, there was no need for them to stroll babies or declutter the floors. Father paid the bills and doled out the discipline. In return, no one questioned mother's culinary and decorative sense; it was what she naturally knew best.

Indeed, in the Moller home, as in most privileged Victorian households, masculine and feminine roles were different but respected in their own right. Thus Lillie's brothers took off their hats to women when they entered their homes and helped them up from sofas. On streetcars, too, they gave up their seats to women of any age and knew never to smoke in their presence. It was the expectation that, when they married, they would provide the standard of living to which genteel ladies had grown accustomed. Lillie, meanwhile, was cultivated to be that genteel lady. To look the part, she dressed "quietly"—no cosmetics and her hair neatly up and tucked back. She never smoked and only in time would be permitted to drink very moderately. She knew to come to breakfast dressed for company, except when she was ill, and to wear a long kimono or "combing jacket" while dressing in her room. Even in privacy, she was told that her guard should never be down.

In public space the rules of engagement were stricter yet. From a very young age, Lillie assisted her mother in her preparations for the outside world, buttoning her mother's gloves at the front door and placing the glove hooks in her purse. Lillie knew to dress with throat, shoulders, and hands covered before opening the front door to meet the world. If she wore an evening dress that exposed more skin, she did not reveal it while in the cab or on the street. She had "completed her toilet" fully, since no adjustments to hair, face, or clothes should be made in view of others. When Lillie walked the street she was expected to look straight ahead at all times; it was unladylike to gawk in windows. One didn't speak to other people unless responding to a direct question. A lady was never to mention a couple's divorce or another woman's pregnancy, unless it was with other women in the privacy of a home. In the rare event a lady was out in mixed company, she was not to be a spectacle—no swearing, flirting, or raucous laughter that made her conspicuous. Annie's rule of thumb was that no woman should allow her name to be uttered in gossip or printed in newspapers—unless it appeared in the births, marriage, or obituary sections. Her mantra, as always, was to leave things to the imagination.

Lillie dreaded the day when she would have to adhere to her parents' very particular rules of engagement with men in public spaces. Older women served as chaperones to young girls attending parties, though, in some cases, when the girl was older than eighteen or engaged, a male escort was permitted. Girls came home immediately after scheduled events and never returned unaccompanied, even if they lived just a block up the road. "Protected" girls didn't so much as mail a letter alone after dark, and those who did appeared bolder than appropriate. Girls who frequently were out and about at night would pay the price later, Lillie's parents warned, for when it was time to accept suitors, no respectable man would think her worthy. To call on a proper woman, a man had to ask a father's permission and respect his wishes if he insisted upon his wife and children being present throughout the courtship. Girls who intervened in the process and spoke to their parents on a suitor's behalf looked overly solicitous, so it generally wasn't done. The goal was to be desired, but not to appear desirous. A proper woman was passive and resigned in matters of love.

If courtships were successful, engagements were supposed to be brief. A serious man needn't flounder about, Annie assured Lillie, just as William hadn't in her case. A marriageable woman, it was thought, was ready in her teens and early twenties, not only for marriage but also to conceive children quickly. Remarriage was generally an acceptable practice in cases when spouses died young. In the Mollers' privileged eyes, however, it was in better taste to remain unmarried after divorce or the death of a spouse—and, in the latter case, mourning should be "universally worn"—that is, never in doubt. Widows wore black in public and were supposed to do little to court suitors within a year of a husband's passing. Lillie understood that if and when she ever married, the suitor should be of her same race, religion, and social class. He need not be of the same age or temperament, however, since it was said that the best matches were with men of opposite disposition of their wives and about five to ten years older. In Lillie's case the hope was to find a confident man to draw her out—an extrovert to compliment her introversion.

Never did Lillie imagine that she would find such a man or be interested in him if she did. In her experience, no boys found her particularly attractive—not that she had given any a chance to know her better. She resigned herself to remaining unmarried, taking care of her mother, and catering to her siblings and their families in time, just as her cousin Tillie did for her aunt Brown and her aunt Brown had done for Grandma Delger. Her resignation to this fate was very upsetting to her mother but less so to her father, since he liked the idea of his oldest daughter at home: "Your mother, aunts, grandmothers, never went to college," he reminded her. "They are cultivated gentlewomen. Your place is here at home, helping your mother and learning to be like her. You can devote yourself to your music, read a lot, travel perhaps."[4] Lillie politely agreed to these terms, since they seemed a better alternative than marrying a virtual stranger who could never understand her.

But she quietly yearned for more—for an intellectual life, later what she would describe as a "rigorous life," a sense of usefulness in the world. Her English teacher had found this greater purpose outside the home, and so had Lillie's godmother and namesake, Aunt Lillie Delger, who was eventually known in the field of psychoanalysis as the respected and pioneering Dr. Lillian Powers. The exploits of this educated, independent aunt were little spoken about in the Moller household, but they increasingly intrigued her bookish niece. Lillie could only gather threads of her aunt's story here and there, but, as more details emerged, they came together in her mind to form a fairy tale different from the one her mother, Annie Moller, was living.

2

College and Adventure

The Sensibilities of a
New Woman, 1896–1904[1]

Coming of age in the 1890s, Lillie Moller was watching the American industrial complex take shape virtually before her eyes. The American Civil War (1861–1865) had catalyzed a technological and industrial boom from which young people of her generation were starting to benefit in their daily quality of life. Whereas the United States had been the fourth leading producer of goods in the world in 1866, by 1900 the nation had risen to first. In the last third of the twentieth century, the economic and cultural climate was ripe for unprecedented innovation; Americans applied for a half million patents for various machines, systems, and processes in the three decades after the war, and many of these innovations allowed for industrial production and distribution to increase exponentially.

The American population was still demographically more rural than urban after the Civil War, but that changed by 1900. New urban centers, even relatively land-locked ones, flourished thanks to better transport methods and the increased use of anthracite coal to fuel factories. In many of these facilities, "efficiency experts" like Frederick Winslow Taylor—a man who will figure prominently in Lillian Gilbreth's life—mechanized production and systematized it with the creation of assembly lines that made companies produce more quickly and efficiently.

With greater production came a need for expanded markets and long-distance communication, which had been made possible by Alexander Graham Bell's invention of the telephone in 1876. Meanwhile, better means of production had led to industrialists wanting to run their businesses and factories for longer hours. The scientists in Thomas Alva Edison's New Jersey lab figured out a solution, developing an incandescent light bulb that burned well into the night.

Wealthy families like Lillie's were able to enjoy these new developments, both as the owners of businesses and as the beneficiaries of electricity and indoor plumbing in their private homes. They, like their goods, could also travel across country more efficiently now than ever before. The urgent need to move troops and supplies during the Civil War had hastened the completion of the Transcontinental Railroad by 1869, connecting the East Coast and West Coast by continuous railroad track. Regional lines branched off of main lines, allowing the US Postal Service to reach nearly all Americans, rural or urban, by 1896. In Lillie's case, the developments in transportation allowed her to travel back and forth between Oakland and New York to see her Moller cousins with once unfathomable regularity. A trip that had taken months by land and weeks by sea, now took a matter of days.

Indeed the systematized railroad system was a development of which Lillie's parents hoped to take full advantage for their daughter's sake. Although she had been raised out West, where her New York relatives thought refinement harder to achieve, her parents hoped that extended trips to the East Coast would compensate for any cultural education their daughter lacked in Oakland. What they had not expected was the extent to which such postwar innovations—railroads, bicycles, domestic gadgets, and the like—would have a liberating effect on girls like their daughter. The technological revolution was one of the primary factors in young women being able to leave the home to engage more fully in public life in the 1890s. With better access to transportation, time-saving devices, and ready-made foods and clothes, women of Lillie's generation were able to focus more intently on leisure, work, and education outside the home. In essence, the Industrial Revolution led to the creation of a "New Woman," one who departed from the domestic ideal of the Victorian age. In time, one of these New Women was Lillie

Moller, whose transformation coincided with her change of name to Lillian Gilbreth.

Of course signs of Lillie's transformation had been there well before she shed her shy exterior. It was becoming clear that young Lillie was at once a homebody and a girl who loved to travel and explore. One of the greatest thrills of her teen years had been in 1893, when her father allowed her to travel east with a schoolmate, stopping along the way in Chicago to attend the highly anticipated World's Fair. Once she reached New York, the Moller cousins took her horseback riding in Central Park and strolling over the newly erected Brooklyn Bridge, the longest suspension bridge in the world. Lillie did not appreciate fully that she had seen an architectural wonder until 1903, when she met her future husband, an architect of wonders of his own. For now, the teenager was far more enraptured by talk of the literary greats who once stood in the places she was standing. On ferries down the Hudson River she invoked the works of Washington Irving and James Fennimore Cooper; traveling north to Boston, she visited the homes of Louisa May Alcott and the transcendental poets, noting the ambiance of the sites more than the architecture. This was where ideas of literary lights germinated and found expression, she thought. Now that she saw what they saw, she wanted to know how it felt to occupy their internal worlds.

Lillie still lost herself in books, but she also grew increasingly fond of music. Her anxiety about playing piano for others eased dramatically in her teen years, so much so that in high school she joined a music society and contemplated a musical career. She showed promise, so her parents indulged her, arranging a private audition with a local composer of note. He took Lillie in, but only under the strictest of terms. Piano had to be her sole priority, he told her. Rather than pursuing formalized study at a conservatory, as talented male musicians would, she trained at home, for only then did she appear appropriately domestic as she practiced to his exacting standards. Lillie complied with his long-term plan for a time, but things came to a head her senior year in high school, when it became apparent that she had other interests, including higher education. Her teacher gave her an ultimatum, and Lillie had to make the uncomfortable break from him—and more importantly, to confront her parents with the admission that she wanted to pursue a college degree.

In all honesty, her parents were not surprised by the admission. Books had brought more joy to this child than to any of their others, and college allowed for more of what she loved. That she remained bookish was a concern to Annie, but less so than it used to be. As high school graduation approached in 1896, Lillie was acting more like the Victorian lady her mother idealized. As the oldest of the Moller girls, she had become a competent caregiver to her siblings and helped her invalid mother run household affairs, thus exhibiting the domestic proclivities that Annie hoped would make her an attractive wife. However, she was increasingly looking outside the home to find fulfillment. Lillie did not fail to notice that young women her age were taking up salaried jobs, athletics, and municipal and social reform activities; a few were even studying to earn college degrees.

Women's engagement with pursuits outside the home was becoming so widespread by the turn of the century that a new form of femininity was coming into view. The ideal woman looked less and less like the Victorian mistress, whose universe was her home. The New Woman participated in politics, higher education, and public life generally. She tried her hand at tennis as well as bicycling, club life, and political lobbying, even though she hadn't yet won the franchise. Increasingly she took in the local nightlife without a chaperone and purchased tickets to sporting events. In time, she even flaunted her sex appeal and admitted her sexual appetite. She was more educated and independent than her mother or grandmother before her.

From what young Lillie could piece together, her unconventional aunt Lillie—the woman so little spoken of in the Moller home—seemed to be a New Woman before anyone thought it acceptable. She had gone off to Europe and married, much like her sister Annie, but from there their paths diverged. Lillie had two baby daughters, who died soon after birth. The tragedies strained her marriage and drove her to look elsewhere for feelings of accomplishment and self-worth. One day she declared that she wanted a divorce and to go to medical school. The Delgers thought that she was being wholly unreasonable, given her age, her gender, her social breeding, and the logistical problem of having none of the prerequisite training behind her. But Aunt Lillie proceeded with her plan anyway and graduated near the top of her class. She fell in love again, this time with another student who supported her career. She moved to New York, but, rather than start another family, she left again for Europe, this time to study psychiatry with the illustrious Sigmund Freud.

Lillie grew up knowing that the Delgers felt disgraced by the divorce and that people generally blamed Aunt Lillie for it. Why, they asked mystified, would she leave a husband still willing to love and protect her? For a time, young Lillie wondered too, only to look back on her judgments and think them "priggish." Now, as she thought about her own pursuits beyond high school graduation, she started to understand and admire Aunt Lillie for seeking her bliss, even if it took her out of the home. Indeed that spring of 1896 Lillie perked up with interest at the news that her cousin Everett Brown was off pursuing his studies at Stanford and that Annie Flo, a female cousin, was allowed to attend the University of California at Berkeley. The latter college had pioneered the higher education of women on the West Coast, and it was close by. Lillie couldn't help but ponder it as a viable option for herself.

The Mollers did not altogether dissuade Lillie from considering an academic career, but they were not completely encouraging either. It was hard to shed their biases about higher education for women. Annie Moller approved of her daughter's intellectual cultivation, but she worried that too much education intimidated potential marriage candidates. William Moller, on the other hand, worried that his daughter's going to college would reflect poorly on him as the patriarch of the family. "College is only necessary for teachers and other women who have to make their living," he reiterated. "No daughter of mine will have to do that."[2] But Lillie desperately *wanted* to earn a living—and rationalized to her parents that she had to be educated not only to become a teacher but also to prepare for the day when she would raise children of her own.

Lillie was wise to argue this way, for it was probably the only rationale Annie and William Moller would accept as valid. Teaching had been a rare acceptable profession for single women of means, at least before they settled down as mothers themselves. William cherished education and hoped that his sons would be college professors or deans when the time came for them to choose careers, but he had more ambivalence about a scholarly path for his daughter, unless properly channeled toward domestic ends. After much deliberation, he and Annie offered a compromise: Lillie could attend nearby Berkeley in the fall of 1896 and then assess the next steps from there. Quietly, the Mollers hoped that over the course of the year their daughter might feel pangs for marriage and motherhood and redirect her energies into a life inside the home.

That the Mollers consented to college at all was an indication that gender norms had softened since Annie had been a teen. It was practically unheard of in her day for American women to attend college. The only institution of higher education that even accepted women before the Civil War, Oberlin College in Ohio, also opened its doors to blacks, making it the most glaring of aberrations until the Seven Sisters opened their doors to women in the 1860s and '70s. The "colleges" and "academies" for women in the postwar decades largely resembled finishing schools like the one Annie attended in Germany, only starting to become serious research centers by the turn of the century, when Lillie became interested in college. Land grant coeducational colleges further west began admitting women too, but female college graduates did not represent a large percentage of the general population. In 1870, less than one percent of American women were college students. By the time Lillie Moller was enrolled at Berkeley, that number had grown to a mere 2.7 percent. The low percentages were attributable to persistent attitudes against the higher education of women but also to the fact that college at the turn of the century, as now, was prohibitively expensive, only a viable option for people with means.

The first generation of American women college students had a qualitatively different experience from men, not just in terms of campus life but also in terms of professional opportunities upon graduation. They had chosen a path of higher education at great sacrifice, for fewer of these women married and had children than was typical in the general population. Apparently higher education and family life were mutually exclusive choices for women with college degrees, for nearly half of this pioneer generation remained single, often supporting themselves. The lucrative fields of law, medicine, business, and politics were almost completely closed to them, thus leaving many to consider underpaid, less prestigious "feminized" fields, such as school teaching or social work in the settlement houses of the nation's industrial cities. Men reasoned that settlement work was appropriate for women because it appeared philanthropic, rather than specialized or scientific, like the purportedly masculine professions. Along with providing health care and social services, settlement workers took on the task of acculturating immigrants to American life. Lillie Moller had glimpses of this work during her rare excursions to Chinatown in San Francisco, where white women tried to teach newly arrived Chinese to read English and prepare Western foods. In New York, Chicago, and Boston, eastern and southern Europeans arrived to immigrant neighborhoods in greater numbers, many of them unskilled and illiterate in English and looking for jobs, training, food, and housing. Settlement work seemed to fill an urgent need for social services in the industrial age, while giving educated women room and board and social purpose. It was not too different, many rationalized, from the pedagogical work women performed at home with children of their own.

Indeed, although it was becoming increasingly acceptable for women to study at university, there was no generalized acceptance of women forging professional careers in culturally masculine fields afterward. This was made abundantly clear at institutions making the reluctant shift to coeducation, Berkeley included. As Lillie enrolled, Benjamin Wheeler, the college president, confirmed his own belief that college learning for women was merely a form of preparation for motherhood. And yet eighteen-year-old Lillie arrived on campus in 1896 anyway, hoping to delay marriage and motherhood, if not to avoid them altogether.

The Berkeley campus was still a work in progress and most definitely a place where women felt like outsiders. As a state university, it waived tuition and entrance fees, but this also meant that it was an institution in perpetual financial crisis. Less well funded than the neighboring private Leland Stanford University, the college consisted of four isolated buildings of varying architecture, equipped with not nearly enough classroom space for the three hundred students matriculating with Lillie that fall. The heiress Phoebe Apperson Hearst, widow of Senator George Hearst and mother of publisher William Randolph Hearst, donated tents to hold classes in, as well as money for scholarships for promising young women. Her support helped, but accommodations for female students remained woefully inadequate. As there were not yet dorms on campus for either sex, students commuted daily and searched for acceptable places to dine and relax in between classes. Men occupied a lunchroom in the basement of North Hall, a venue too raucous for students who thought themselves respectable women.

When Lillie wanted to study, she found little nooks on campus where she could sit undisturbed. She took her share of liberal arts courses—logic, philosophy, the history of philosophy, ethics, and aesthetics—and studied Virgil, Cicero, and Kant. To appease her parents she kept up her German, all the while winning prizes for sonnets submitted to the campus literary magazine. In this intellectual environment she had a markedly easier time making friends than at any other time in her life, and her parents were stunned by her social transformation. The Theta sorority, a women's social organization that had opened a chapter at Berkeley in 1890, invited Lillie to join, but she graciously declined to devote more time to writing and theater. Annie accepted Lillie's choice, since she was coming out of her shell in so many other ways. Within her first year on campus, she won the lead in a play directed by faculty in the English department.

These years of growth for Lillie were hard to reconcile with developments in the Moller household, however. While Annie's eldest child was debuting on the Berkeley stage, she was indisposed, giving birth to yet another child—her third and last boy. The contrast between mother and daughter was startling: Annie had resigned herself to perpetual domesticity, as Lillie transgressed the boundaries of that circumscribed world. Although Annie had once been discouraged from fraternizing with any man she didn't intend to marry, her daughter interacted more and more with men who were not potential suitors—but they were men who respected her mind. Several brothers of the Phi Delta Theta fraternity house had become her trusted friends; they told her that they did not consider her brains "a handicap" as her mother worried they might. Lillie breathed a sigh of relief to know that she finally was being accepted on her terms.

In fact, during her four years at Berkeley, Lillie performed so well in her classes that President Wheeler chose her as one of three students to speak at the graduation ceremony in 1900. Several of her professors offered advice for the occasion: be womanly in your presentation, they warned; don't try to imitate the male speakers. Lillie took the advice to heart, choosing to wear a dress with accentuated ruffles draped over the neckline of her graduation robe. Indeed she looked determinedly feminine as she approached the lectern of the Herman Gymnasium to speak on "Life—A Means or an End." Although their daughter had stayed at university longer than they had hoped, Annie and William Moller beamed at the ceremony and afterward, as people approached them and complimented their raising of a daughter so perfectly composed. On this occasion Lillie was to break one of her mother's cardinal rules, having her name mentioned in the newspaper for something other than a birth, a marriage, or a death. This once pathologically shy daughter was being heralded for an inspired speech, as well as for finishing at the top of her class with an English degree.

Even the most casual observer could see that the young woman who graduated in 1900 was altogether different from the reclusive child she once had been. At her high school graduation four years earlier, she had appeared uncomfortable in her skin, undone when it was brought to her attention that she had dressed for the occasion slightly unlike the other girls. But photographs of the college graduate after the ceremonies betray a new self-assuredness. Rather than be encumbered by yards of crinoline like the Victorian woman of old, she donned a more masculine, broad-shouldered suit jacket to outline the contours of her tall, slender frame. If the transformation wasn't already fully apparent on her sleeve, it was obvious in her change of name. She asked that she no longer be referred to as the delicate "Lillie" but rather the more sophisticated "Lillian," just like her aunt, the psychoanalyst Lillian Powers.

College life opened up intellectual vistas, but there was that tinge of doubt about men's intentions for her: How seriously did they take her in the academic world? In the back of her mind, she wondered if the invitation to speak at graduation was a consolation prize for not being chosen for the Phi Beta Kappa honorary society, an honor she desperately wanted and thought she deserved. She had heard that the final slot in the society was going to her, but members decided at the eleventh hour to offer it to a male student, who they figured would need the boasting rights for employment purposes more than a woman ever would. Apparently Berkeley men presumed that Lillian had worked hard to be nothing more than an exemplar of enlightened motherhood, a view commensurate with the expectations of her back home. After the excitement of graduation subsided, talk in the Moller household was not about Lillian finding employment but about how she could be reintegrated back into the household. Her sisters were getting older and needed chaperones to society events, Annie reminded her, and the boys needed a nanny she could trust. Lillian implicitly understood that these obligations were hers after her four-year hiatus from domestic duties, and she reluctantly returned to fulfill them.

The transition would have been easier had Lillian not witnessed other women at Berkeley moving on to pursue their doctorate degrees. There was Millicent Washburn Shinn, for example, who studied the sensory development of infants; and Jessica Peixotto, who earned her PhD in the department of political science. Clearly the idea of graduate degrees for women was not unprecedented, and yet it was not so common that Lillian felt confident making the case to her parents. Discreetly she talked with her literature professor Charles Gayley about pursuing a graduate degree in English. If she could, he advised, she should go to New York City to study with James Brander Matthews, a renowned scholar of literature at Columbia University.

When Lillian finally broached the subject with her parents, it was all much the same as before. They did not object in theory to her traveling, particularly to New York, where the Moller relatives could monitor her movements. But there was that ever-present fear that their daughter was making herself a less and less attractive wife as time wore on and degrees accrued. Lillian tried to assuage their fears. The subjects that interested her most, she assured them, were philosophy and literature, fields deemed more feminine than most. Men would see her knowledge of them as evidence of refinement, not of careerism; she would be endearing, not intimidating in their eyes. Nothing her parents could say would diminish her resolve, and so the Mollers reluctantly agreed to let her study at Columbia in the fall of 1900, hoping that her excursion east would bring her back home in a year. Perhaps with the gentle prodding of the Mollers in New York, they hoped, she might meet a man with whom she'd want to settle into married life.

Lillian was twenty-two when she left for New York and still not permitted to travel unchaperoned. William Moller accompanied his daughter and installed her in the women's dormitory at Barnard, the sister school of Columbia. Although women could not attend Columbia as undergraduates, nearly half of its graduate school was female, and thus she was in good company. Few of the women she met expected to earn a living as a scholar; they were merely biding time, holding out a bit longer until they could find suitors of mutual liking. Their chastity and moral virtue had to be carefully preserved in the meantime, and thus parents took comfort in knowing that their daughters returned to a women's dorm after hours, their extracurricular movements watched by dorm matrons. Administrators, like parents, prodded them into courses of study with domestic bents, such as home economics or pedagogy. It made more sense, in their minds, to cultivate arts and skills needed to raise children and keep a home, as this was likely going to be their vocation in the longer term.

Lillian's first semester did not proceed as she had hoped. Once she settled in the dorm and met with Professor Matthews, it became clear that he had no intention of working with her, or any woman for that matter. Regardless of the university's policy of admitting women graduate students, it was Matthews' personal policy to refuse them. Much later Lillian found a silver lining in his chauvinism, but it was a long time coming and not before some desperate scrambling to figure out her next move. The thought of her father returning to New York to take her home was too humiliating to contemplate.

But all was not lost in looking elsewhere in the university for mentors, given the international well of scholars from which to draw. Lillian's first love had always been literature, and it was a field her parents had tacitly approved. But at Berkeley she had also been exposed to other fields—newer fields, in which women had not yet the experience or visibility to establish themselves. Her aunt was one of the first women to break into psychoanalysis, the discipline founded by Sigmund Freud in the late 1800s, for which she needed a medical degree. Lillian wasn't interested in getting a medical degree, but she had always been fascinated by the human mind. She took psychology and philosophy at Berkeley, hoping to garner some understanding of human motivation— her own and other people's. Why did some women want husbands more than others? Why, in her case, was a married life at home not enough? What was it that motivated her to go to graduate school and be productive beyond the traditional sense for women? What was it, more generally, that drove some people to work harder than others? This curiosity about human motivation would form the basis for much of her research and writing in her later career.

In time, Lillian regrouped and found a more amenable home in Columbia's Department of Psychology. Most influential among the faculty was Edward Thorndike, a young, newly appointed instructor whose ideas about human motivation and learning informed her work forever after. Thorndike made Lillian think of human psychology as relative rather than universal; dynamic, not fixed. She too came to believe that individuals are shaped to some degree by their *environment*, and that their sense of satisfaction and fulfillment in work is derived from factors that differ from person to person. In an age of mass production, the idea that workers were *individuals* went against the grain. Certainly the leading lights of the industrial efficiency movement, Frederick Winslow Taylor most notably, treated employees as if they were one and the same; the standardization of positions and tasks was, Taylor insisted, the key to producing more efficiently with higher profits. The meat packing industry, as one of many, had been revolutionized, for better or worse, when human workers were put on an assembly line and made to execute the same exact cutting and hauling movements over and over again. But Thorndike convinced Lillie that such work was not necessarily sustaining to all people at all times, that human beings' skills and motivations changed over time and context. There was indeed a *psychology* to being productive in the mechanized age.

Thorndike's influence was the silver lining in Lillian's New York experience, but it came to an abrupt end. It surprised her that she grew homesick, but she did, and it led to physical symptoms that were debilitating at times. The New York Mollers were worried, and they took her in. Spending more and more time with her cousins, Lillian made little effort to befriend others in the dorm, but of course the living arrangements had never been to her liking anyway. The housing office hadn't paired her with a serious graduate student but rather with a messy undergraduate girl whose belongings took over the room. Lillian's response was the one she had known as a child: to turn inward, spending most of her time reading books. Her cousins worried that she studied too obsessively; so wrapped up in her subjects, Lillian was skipping meals and growing thin. She was also utterly unprepared for the New York winter and fell sick with the cold weather. The Mollers urged William to return east to retrieve his daughter, which he promptly did. Her excursion to graduate school looked to be a bust.

Lillian's almost immediate recovery upon her return to Oakland made her realize just how much comfort she had always taken in family and familiar surroundings. Annie could not have been more pleased that her daughter was home; perhaps her failed attempt at graduate school and independent living was the jolt she needed to readjust to the domestic life intended for her. But this was not what Lillian took away from the experience. When her depression lifted and she felt more like herself, she refocused on academic goals. Now, she was stronger and more determined, she decided. She wanted to return to graduate school, this time just closer to home. Annie's hopes for her daughter were deferred yet again.

In August of 1901 Lillian registered for graduate courses at Berkeley. She took education and philosophy courses and planned to write a master's thesis in Elizabethan literature, this time under her old mentor Charles Gayley. It surprised him when she chose as her topic Ben Jonson's *Bartholomew Fair*, a play considered racy for its commentary on social caste and religious conflict in Medieval England. Lillian admitted that the playwright exhibited more frankness than would have been deemed appropriate "in real life," but that was what intrigued her about him. Jonson's unspoken truths found voice on the page, and for her, too, the realm of written words was a safe place to engage thoughts that were too unconventional to utter in proper society. In her writing, she could experiment, question, and escape without detection. She wanted to do it more, and, after receiving her master's degree in English in the spring of 1902, she contemplated a doctorate degree.

Annie permitted more schooling, but only because her daughter was finally coming around in other ways. It was as if the contemplation of unladylike topics in her studies had provided Lillian a release of pent-up thoughts and emotions that allowed her to return to her mother's world of refinement. She knew that her mother wanted her to assume her role as a cultured lady, and she did it willingly, seeming to take pleasure in the art of preening like other women her age. Her activities in and outside the classroom were better balanced in Annie's eyes, for her daughter studied and then left campus to buy hats and handbags for Saturday matinees and operas downtown. Friends remarked that with her slim figure, coiffed hair, and tailored suits she was a modern sight to behold. Her fashion sense reflected the more liberated life she and so many young women of her generation were leading, compared to the cloistered existence of their mothers. Corsets loosened and dress hems rose to accommodate their increased physicality in public space. Once encumbered by yards of fabric, modern women chose more practical A-lined frocks and simpler hairstyles that resembled the fashion plates drawn by the artist Charles Dana Gibson for *Scribner's* and other popular magazines of the era. Smart and quietly unconventional, Lillian Gilbreth could not help but seize on changing sensibilities about women's appropriate realms of influence—and it showed. In her early twenties, people remarked that she looked like a Gibson girl in the flesh.

As so many of her fashionable friends were doing, she even decided to take an extensive trip to Europe before embarking on her doctoral studies; two former schoolmates from San Francisco planned to join her before being betrothed. It may seem odd that parents so cautious to chaperone their daughters locally would let them travel in Europe for months at a time, but such excursions were rites of passage in elite society—accepted, even expected, practice for ladies who hoped to cultivate themselves before marrying. Hundreds of thousands of privileged American men and women at the turn of the century considered an extended trip to Europe an absolute requisite of their cultural education, much as Annie Moller's parents thought it for hers.

And yet these excursions had alternative meanings for the young women embarking on them, too: they provided a socially sanctioned way to break away from domestic life for a time to experience independence. In the case of the famed reformer Jane Addams, her trip to Europe in the late 1880s had served to give her a sense of social purpose in the world, for it opened her eyes to the settlement work she pioneered when she returned to Chicago in 1889. For Lillian's San Francisco contemporary Gertrude Stein, Paris became home in 1903 as well as a site of sexual liberation and rebellion. Lillian had no plans to break the mold, but she hoped, if nothing else, to clear her head to contemplate what her undecided future would hold. The Mollers were giving her freedom, an opportunity to work through her underlying anxieties about the unknown. She still was unsure whether her graduate studies would lead to a career, or whether she ever wanted to marry.

Of course, this freedom had limits. The young women would not be jaunting off completely on their own, since their parents found a cultured chaperone to accompanying them, a teacher of Latin and Greek at Oakland High School by the name of Minnie Bunker. She was a forty-five-year-old spinster, who had come to supervise women abroad as a way of paying her expenses. The Mollers saw in her all that they hoped Lillian would be if, heaven forbid, she hadn't the greater fortune of finding a husband: she was neat, proper, and had an expert knowledge of art and literature that made her useful for cultivating younger women coming of age. The plan for the lady travelers was to arrive in New York to take in the sights for a few days and then to tour historic Boston before setting off overseas. For Lillian, it was the ninth time she had been to the East Coast; for her friends, the trip was their first.

In Boston, Minnie tried to make her charges feel less homesick by introducing them to her relatives—true New England Yankees from Fairfield, Maine. Aunt Martha was a widow, and her two daughters, Minnie's cousins, were women of surprising intellect and professional acclaim. One was a renowned biologist whose specimens had been donated to the botany museum of Harvard; the other, a world-class musician, lived nearby with her family in Brookline. Lillian had met few women like them or families so supportive of their professional endeavors. Aunt Martha Bunker, a former schoolmistress, lived with her sister Aunt Kit and had long been a widow. The man of their house was Martha's only son Frank Bunker Gilbreth, the clear center of attention for all the Bunker women.

When Lillian met Frank Gilbreth on the steps of the Boston Public Library that summer in 1903, she walked away with a strong but perplexing first impression. He was extroverted, clearly well fed, and decidedly "all boy." Although he sounded relatively well read and worldly, he wasn't college trained, nor did he work in a traditional white-collar occupation. According to Minnie, Cousin Frank was a self-made man, who had worked his way up in the gritty world of construction to make a name for himself. Just shy of seventeen, he had been poised to enter the Massachusetts Institute of Technology (MIT), but studying didn't appeal to him. He became a bricklayer's apprentice instead and took mechanical engineering courses at night; within two years he was a foreman, two years later a superintendent. As he mastered the bricklaying trade he developed techniques for handling corners more quickly, and soon he built rigging to minimize needless movement and lifting. Traditional methods required as many as eighteen compartmentalized movements to lay a brick; Frank Gilbreth had whittled them down to five, allowing a man to double his hourly yield. After patenting his adjustable scaffold, he invented concrete mixers, conveyors, and apparatus that allowed him to build houses, mills, canals, skyscrapers, and basic infrastructure of whole towns in record speed. By 1895 he headed his own construction company and went back to MIT—this time to build its electrical laboratory in a mere eleven weeks.[3]

The stories about him were impressive, but Lillian couldn't see that she had much in common with this confident man. She was a tall, reedy society girl breaking away from her cloistered life; Frank was a hefty man ten years her senior and discernibly rough around the edges. She was a devout Lutheran, but Frank had long been dubious of organized religion, insisting that the observation of rites was no indication of one's spirituality. He liked to think that he had arrived at his sense of morality on his own and boasted about it along with his self-made success. Lillian, meanwhile, remained reserved and understated, having been taught not to draw attention to deficits or assets that should instead announce themselves. Still, she found something surprisingly charming about this man. Perhaps it was his banter or his gentle, sloping eyelids, a trait, she soon discovered, that was shared by several other Bunker relatives. Lillian thought Frank Gilbreth larger than life, and yet he talked to her without insulting her intelligence. She imagined that the way he bragged to her was much the way he engaged any of the men he met on his construction sites.[4]

Minnie invited her young charges to join Cousin Frank for a ride in his red Winton Six Coaching Car. Lillian agreed to go but again was left with a mixed impression. Both the car and its driver were flashy, to be sure; the vehicle was three times more expensive than the standard Model T Ford, and Frank seemed to think that his female riders should be utterly fascinated by what was underneath its hood. The ladies indulged him before they suggested touring the grounds of Harvard and nearby colleges. Frank decided that a tour of the city's newer architecture would be more exciting, especially one that featured structures of his own design. He drove from site to site, speaking of technical aspects of construction that Lillian new nothing about. He tried to draw her out by asking about the buildings of San Francisco, even some in Oakland, but she could only concede that she rarely noticed buildings with no history—they hadn't yet earned their cultural value. No matter how much effort each made to engage the other on his or her terms, it was clear that Frank knew as little about high art as she knew about constructing buildings. It remained an awkward scene until a blown tire provided a common topic of conversation. Frank was embarrassed, but it oddly broke the ice; Lillian preferred the more vulnerable man now before her and looked forward to seeing more of him during her short stay in Boston.

The night before embarking for Europe, Lillian dined out with the Bunkers and her companions. She was surprised to feel so awkward in Frank's presence. It frustrated her that no humorous quips came to mind to counter his constant teasing; he seemed to enjoy keeping her flustered, and yet she was intrigued by the challenge of him. For all his joking, he wanted to know what Lillian thought about things, some of which she had never considered. He had a fascination with Egyptian relics and posited theories on the transmigration of souls after death. As they talked through the night, Minnie Bunker could see that there was a mutual attraction, and she grew leery. As charming as Frank could be, she did not think him a suitable match for a woman like Lillian Moller. Frank was successful, but not refined; Lillian was educated, but largely ignorant to the ways of the world. Because so much of Frank's learning had occurred in the proverbial school of life, Minnie worried that he and Lillian had little by way of common experience. Frank had been self-sufficient too long to cater to the preferences of other people; she wondered if any woman, in fact, was accommodating enough to handle a man like her cousin.

The next morning Frank accompanied the ladies to the dock where the steamer awaited passengers, and he helped Lillian get installed in her stateroom. He considered telling her of his growing feelings for her but then thought it best to say nothing; he would wait to see how she felt about him when she returned in November. Lillian, too, was thinking intensely about Frank but keeping it to herself. Her companions were too preoccupied with their own circumstances to notice; one mulled over an offer of marriage, while the other seemed to be in a perpetual state of writing or waiting for letters from her betrothed. But Minnie couldn't hide her matronly concern and discreetly took Lillian aside. Her warnings about Frank were not encouraging; he was charming, she agreed, but also utterly devoted to his mother. She went on to weave an intricate story about another woman who had passed away and with whom no one else would ever compete for a place in Frank's heart. Lillian did not suspect that the details of this story were fabricated, and thus Minnie accomplished her purpose: if Lillian had any hopes that Frank was interested in her, they were almost completely dashed. Nevertheless, Frank vowed that he would be waiting on the dock when she returned in four months' time; Lillian told herself that if he kept his promise and met her on the dock, it would prove his serious intentions.

Thankfully, she had many wonderful diversions over the next several months. The ladies journeyed from Edinburgh to Westminster Abbey and then across the channel to France, Holland, Belgium, Switzerland, Austria, and Italy. Minnie planned the itinerary to the hour: lectures and museums in the mornings, excursions in the afternoons, and concerts and plays in the evenings, with occasional breaks to shop. Lillian partook in the fashionable society of Vienna as her mother would have hoped, and she stood uncomfortably for fittings of suits and hats. She left the others briefly to meet up with Moller cousins in Berlin and attended a Wagner opera in Munich. The independence was liberating; she had so much time by herself just to think. Sometimes she contemplated the doctoral work that lay ahead, but, more urgently, she wondered if Frank Gilbreth would appear on the dock when she arrived in Boston in November.

3

The Gilbreths' Brand of Companionate Marriage, 1904–1908[1]

As it turned out, Frank kept his promise. From the boat Lillian caught sight of him standing alongside the Mollers to help her disembark. He was all smiles and pleasantries, admitting only later that he was hiding secrets. While Lillian was away, he grew violently ill, and surgeons performed an emergency appendectomy, a life-threatening procedure, only weeks before her return. He didn't want to create undue anxiety for the women abroad, and thus he said nothing about it. A man who exhibited much bravado months before now teased less and tread lightly; new emotions ran through him that made him uncharacteristically vulnerable, easily bruised. Rather than write Lillian directly in Europe, he had sent postcards addressed to all of her travel companions so that his attentions looked evenly spread. He knew that Minnie detected his designs and likely disapproved of them.

But it was readily apparent to the Bunkers and Mollers that Frank and Lillian's feelings were mutual. Immediately upon her return he took Lillian to the Metropolitan Museum of Art to explore its Egyptian wing and then to his office to meet his business partners and Anne Bowley, his indispensable secretary. For the first time he walked and talked with her alone, and she seemed amenable to all of his plans. That night, he invited her family to his home before attending a theatrical production of *The Wizard of Oz*. Frank and Lillian sat separately by themselves, and no one openly expressed disapproval. It had become increasingly permissible to allow young people to get to know each other more personally before marriage. Not only were women of Lillian's generation spending more time in public places, enjoying theaters, restaurants, and sporting events in mixed company, they were also being more expressive of their romantic interests. Lillian, a twenty-five-year-old college graduate, enjoyed fewer restrictions than her mother, who at her age was already married with children. By no means was it acceptable to date multiple suitors casually, but the Mollers did not object to their daughter spending time with a man who might be a husband in due time. They could see that their daughter was interested in Frank Gilbreth like no one else before him.

After several days in Boston, Frank and Lillian went their separate ways—Frank staying east and Lillian returning to the West Coast. They had a fortuitous opportunity to meet up again in Chicago weeks later, as Frank had business prospects there and Lillian was traveling with the Mollers. It was on this occasion that Frank boldly asked if he could take Lillian alone to see a play, and that Annie surprisingly voiced no objections. When Lillian returned to Oakland for the winter holidays, Frank managed to create yet another occasion for "stopping in" while en route to clients in Seattle. Lillian was excited and nervous at once: on this occasion her siblings would get the chance to inspect the man who they all acknowledged was her first serious suitor.

Christmas was a bigger test than Frank likely knew: the Mollers were an insular clan, and they wondered amongst themselves how this self-assured Yankee would fall in with the rest. If William and Annie had any apprehensions, they could also see that Lillian, the child most protective of family rituals, wanted Frank Gilbreth to be part of her most intimate world. The day after Christmas all the Delger and Brown cousins headed out for a tour of San Francisco, which gave the couple a chance to walk and talk alone. Thanks to Frank, Lillian saw the city anew—not merely as a cultural center but also as an architectural metropolis. Writing to his mother about the day, Frank noted gratefully that Annie Moller had been cordial and accommodating beyond what likely made her comfortable, even permitting her daughter to accompany him on the boardwalk of the Golden Gate Bridge. Frank thought nothing more appropriate than to ask Lillian to marry him on one of the greatest engineering wonders he had ever seen.

Then and there, Lillian came to understand much about her future husband, including his penchant for efficiency. The temporary engagement ring he had chosen for her had already been engraved with the date of their excursion on the Golden Gate Bridge. Apparently her acceptance of his proposal was yet another instance of everything conforming to plan. But there were other things about Frank Gilbreth she would come to understand only after accepting his proposal and, implicitly, the strenuous life that he had in mind for them. That he sought her approval in marriage before he sought William Moller's was, she hoped, an indication of how Frank would proceed in the future—to treat Lillian as a partner, rather than a child, a trophy, or a drudge. Indeed she would discover that this was true, albeit to a greater extent than she could have imagined.

Shortly after his marriage proposal Frank gave Lillian a diamond ring from Tiffany's in New York City, but he could not give it in person. His brain raced with too many ideas not to get started on them right away, he told her, and thus he headed back East to generate new business, warning her that he likely would not see her again until their wedding in ten months' time, in October of 1904. Lillian held off wearing the ring or sending out official announcements: a proper woman said nothing publicly of a marriage proposal until her family endorsed the union, and, in all honesty, she did not yet know what the Mollers' reaction would be. Frank hadn't formally sought their consent first, and the Mollers had their preferences for the traditional.

The Mollers believed Frank loved Lillian, but they did not know if they truly approved of him. He seemed to have an unlimited amount of energy that needed outlets, and thus he never sat still for long. Although there was something admirable about his go-getting spirit and his self-made success, the Mollers also thought there was something disturbing about his abandon. They worried that his hasty departure from San Francisco was a sign of his rash decision-making and possibly the root of financial instability to come. He had an all-or-nothing mentality when it came to investments; although he had enjoyed great gains, he also suffered volatile shifts in the market that had brought him, they found out later, to the brink of bankruptcy on more than one occasion. The Mollers worried that their daughter was being exploited and marrying beneath her, relinquishing the protection and privilege to which women of her class were accustomed. Would this Yankee upstart be able to provide for Lillian at all times? When they looked at their beaming daughter, they could not help but give Frank the benefit of the doubt.

In their months apart, Frank sent his fiancée manuscripts to prepare for publication and advertising brochures to critique, just as a business partner would. Lillian responded by mailing him a copy of Walter Dill Scott's *The Theory of Advertising*, a book she had read under Thorndike and thought might enhance Frank's understanding of the power of emotional appeals. Proud as he was to call himself self-taught, Frank proved receptive to her perspectives on psychology and trusted her judgment as an editor of his work. He saw her as such an asset that he even sent Lillian the work he considered his masterpiece, a booklet called "Field System," to overhaul for publication. In finding a future wife, he also apparently discovered a complement to his work that had been missing up until then.

Annie Moller could see that her daughter was taking an interest in Frank's construction business, as she corresponded back and forth about it with him throughout their engagement. Yet Lillian's enthusiasm for such things was unbefitting a proper lady, as Annie saw it. She had never so much as inquired about the business dealings of her husband, nor had her mother before her, causing her to view Frank as an uncouth influence. Lillian had seriously considered living by her parents' preferences, being the dutiful daughter in their home until marrying a respectable man and catering to his domestic needs. But she wanted something more—usefulness within as well as outside the home. Frank Gilbreth wanted this multifaceted life for Lillian, and, yes, expected it to some degree.

The Mollers tried to suspend judgment, for, despite being preoccupied in Frank's affairs, Lillian was performing her social duties to perfection. That winter her name did not appear on a graduate school roster but rather in the local society pages, with her discerning mother's approval; journalists noted her presence about town attending parties and donning the latest Paris fashions. In the summer months she dutifully watched over her younger siblings at the Mollers' summer cottage and prepared for the receptions and showers organized in her honor. The engagement tea that Annie planned for the fall was to be the most spectacular of them all—specially ordered flowers and tailored outfits from abroad, to go with a guest list of four hundred of San Francisco's elite.

The social plans betrayed the glaringly different sensibilities of Lillian's family and her husband-to-be. This was a world in which Frank Gilbreth felt conspicuously out of place, and Lillian sensed it. In letters back and forth he fussed over the pictures she chose to display at her engagement parties, fearing that they would sour her friends and family before he arrived for the wedding. He doubted that photographic likeness did him justice. To associates in Boston, he presented himself as all confidence, and he was; his Puritan stock held currency there when he boasted of his family tree, for he was a descendant of one of the original founders of Harvard College. In New England, his lineage seemed to explain his reputation for thrift and hard work. But it did nothing to transform the photograph that stood on display for the Mollers' acquaintances, friends, and family in Oakland. On first inspection, they might see him as discernibly older but not necessarily more distinguished and perhaps even ill refined. At five feet, nine inches tall and over two hundred pounds, he looked stout next to his willowy bride to be. Lillian comforted him with assurances that her siblings and cousins seemed to like him and that one of her former teachers described him as more vigorous and handsome than the professor type she presumed her star pupil would marry, if she married at all. *She* was the one out of her element, she reminded Frank. He had nothing to fear.

When he arrived in Oakland, Frank tried his best to do the Mollers proud at the events they planned in his honor, but quietly he let it be known that his preference was for an understated wedding, an occasion to match the simplicity of his upbringing. Avoiding all potential ostentation, Martha Gilbreth decided it best to forego the spectacle of her son's wedding and didn't attend, waiting instead for Frank's return to the East Coast after the honeymoon. Indeed, he had decided that New

York was where they would start their new life together, and Lillian seemed to acquiesce to his plan willingly, perhaps anxious to break free of the Moller stronghold and her cloistered way of life. Annie's irritation at her daughter's quiet rebellion was obvious, as was her disappointment over not throwing a wedding extravaganza to remember. Grudgingly, she respected Frank's wishes to have a private affair, which she held in her home on an uneventful Wednesday evening. Lillian's five sisters were her bridesmaids, and her cousin Everett Brown was Frank's best man. Aside from two of Lillian's girlfriends, cousins and grandparents were the only others present for the ceremony.

After the wedding supper the couple took a suite at the St. Francis Hotel in San Francisco's Union Square and left the next morning on a train to their honeymoon destination, the World's Fair in St. Louis. One of Lillian's young brothers saw them off, and family friends accompanied them on the train for part of the way, curiously watching the new couple interact. Frank seemed unfazed by the scrutiny or by the fact that strangers came to look upon them curiously, too, as the train trudged eastward. In fact he proceeded to apprentice his wife right there in the coach car, pulling out pen and paper to offer Lillian lessons in masonry. He knew nothing about Elizabethan literature, he reminded her, and thus it only made sense to him that she learn his trade rather than he learn hers. Lillian knew nothing about engineering, but she was far more amenable to being an apprentice. From this point forward, she, more often than he, bent to the whims of the other.

The honeymoon trip was productive from a professional standpoint and more. It is likely that Frank and Lillian conceived their first child in St. Louis, and the time alone gave them an opportunity to discover each other's assets both as business partners and life partners. Formal as it seemed, Frank requested that his new wife submit to him a list of qualifications she brought to the partnership—a "job analysis" she later likened to the "surveying and outfitting" performed by an engineer as he first meets a client. Like any engineering contract, he explained, their marriage required an assessment of assets so that the partners could "meet the world as a firm."

It appeared that Frank was designing a marriage to suit him, and in the beginning Lillian might have agreed. Although Frank wanted a partnership in business and parenting, he insisted that Martha and Aunt Kit have authority over most domestic affairs in his home. In his thirty-six years of bachelorhood, he had never suffered from womanly neglect, and he saw no reason to relinquish the attentions of the Bunker women as a married man. Lillian marveled at how the Bunker women doted on her husband, never asking him to raise a finger. After a day's work he always returned to "a smiling welcome, a bountifully spread table, keen admiration," she later noted, amused. Why would he want to give it up?

It wasn't as if Lillian hadn't been warned that her mother-in-law and her sister would be a part of her new household. During her honeymoon, Frank's "duplicate mothers" were busy finding a suitable apartment on the Upper West Side of Manhattan for all four of them to occupy. The Bunker women had already furnished and decorated it by the time Lillian first stepped foot in it, forcing her to put her personal items in storage. When all four housemates sat at their first meal as a family, Martha placed a chair at the head of the table for Lillian, but Lillian demurred and sat elsewhere, much to Frank's approval. He still saw his mother as mistress of the house and stipulated that she do all the cooking, since it was what he had always known. Lillian understood that she should make herself scarce on rare nights he was home for dinner so that he could spend an hour alone with his mother.

On his frequent business trips to Boston, Frank left his new wife to fend for herself with the older housemates. Sometimes they were so domineering that they reduced her to tears. She longed to be useful, but Martha had her own domestic system in place and refused her daughter-in-law's assistance, preferring to hire out domestics to tend to laundry and cleaning to her specifications. It never occurred to Frank that, as the women jockeyed for primacy in his household, his wife might resent the situation. But Lillian eventually looked back at these stressful first months of marriage and saw them as a blessing in disguise. Indeed Martha's influence in the household could be oppressive, but it liberated her in ways few wives of her generation ever knew. Unburdened by cooking, cleaning, or darning socks, Lillian was freed up to throw herself into motherhood and the professional work Frank expected of her outside the home. No one criticized Lillian for neglecting her domestic duties, since Martha and Kit tended to them happily and with the greatest of care.

It also helped that women in other American households were experiencing similar sorts of liberation. Motherhood remained an expectation for them, but more women with college degrees also attempted to combine marriage and education, children and career, unlike the degree-holding women before them. Technological advancements had freed them from much of the domestic drudgery of previous generations of homemakers, too; thus, rather than spending hours making clothes and preserving food, for instance, they bought ready-made fashions, breads, and canned goods and spent the time left over to partake in a profession or leisure activities outside the home. Thanks to new technologies, as well Martha's added assistance, Lillian could focus more intently on her apprenticeships in motherhood and the building trade.

Some might say that Frank's preferences resembled a "companionate marriage," a union in which a couple enjoyed mutual sexual attraction, respect, and emotional support. This arrangement was increasingly the preference in the modern age: in marriage, as well as out, Americans acknowledged women more and more as sexual beings who in fact desired sexual gratification unattached to procreation. Back in the 1870s the suffragist Elizabeth Cady Stanton seemed heretical when she openly questioned the Victorian presumption that women were strictly maternal and naturally asexual, interested in intercourse merely to fulfill the destiny of conceiving babies. Americans of Annie Moller's generation rejected Stanton's notion of "self-sovereignty," the simple idea that women had the right to control their own bodies in marriage. Lillian's generation would be far more receptive to Stanton's call for "voluntary motherhood"—married women's right to say no to sex if they did not want to conceive. One piece of evidence is the simple fact that the number of children born to American families declined: whereas American women bore more than seven children on average in 1800, by 1900 that number had nearly halved.

Certainly families had less of a need for children as more of them moved from farms to cities by 1900 and had fewer physical chores, but this decline in number also speaks to the cultural preferences of women to raise fewer children, either to pursue more activities outside the home or to dote more intently on the children they already had. Of course none of these changing sensibilities about sex and procreation explains the choices Lillian Gilbreth made in her life, which leads one to speculate again at the extent to which her choices were entirely hers. How much did she want to work outside the home and raise a brood of children at once?

The evidence answering this question is slim and suggests strongly that her choices were Frank's. Two of her children later insisted that it was their father's decision to have a dozen children as well as to run a family business. And yet, for all the apparent one-sidedness in their marriage, it is worth considering what Lillian got out of Frank's master plan. Although she reflected little about her hectic life in writing, there is reason to believe that she wanted to do what she did and did not regret it afterward. So many factors likely came into play: She loved children as well as learning; she admired her mother's domestic role but wanted to rebel from it too. She wanted to please her husband, but she also had a deep-seated desire to succeed in something at which she excelled. Like all women, she was multifaceted, with hopes and desires that others told her were incommensurate with each other. During her decades of wifedom and early motherhood, she sought to make them compatible. She acquiesced to Frank's whims, and yet she likely never thought herself a sufferer of them. His ambitions allowed her to avoid much of the drudgery of domestic life. He was essentially giving her a ticket out of the home and paying her entry into other spheres of endeavor where she would not be permitted without him. She was willing to learn about her husband's masculine field because it was work that society viewed as important and it stimulated her mind. She was too polite to admit that she had professional ambitions too, but quietly she must have. In time Frank saw that she was well suited to his work, virtually redefining it in his name.

And thus the Gilbreth marriage grew to be more complex than any etiquette book prescribed at the time. Never was it an autocracy, nor could it be, since Frank was away on business too often to be a lording presence. Lillian necessarily ran both business and household much of the time. But their "partnership" was also not the democracy that a partnership suggests. More times than not, Frank gave orders, and Lillian carried them out in his absence. When she disagreed with his dictums, she rarely questioned him in front of others. Several of the Gilbreth children and caretakers recalled years later that there were days when Lillian took herself off to cry or expressed displeasure under her breath—indeed she felt deep frustration in being overruled. But no one knows of this frustration because of Lillian's own admissions. That she didn't object loudly to Frank's plans or confess resentment in her writings suggests that she still internalized lingering notions about a woman's place. She was to be seen, not heard; she was to follow, not initiate; she was to learn, not teach—at least not conspicuously. It is likely that she also felt quite torn. Frank demanded, but Frank also sanctioned her working outside the home in ways her contemporaries never could, since their husbands would have forbidden it.

Although Lillian never made this known publicly, it is also likely that she didn't complain because she found subtle ways to exert her influence anyway, without seeming to overstep the bounds of feminine propriety. The proof is not in words but in outcomes. Her power came with time and experience, as she learned that Frank was less receptive to her views when confronted directly or made to look wrong in front of others. Although Frank presented the final word to clients and children, his wife had more and more say in private deliberations; she had his ear, because she had proven that she was instinctive and trustworthy. Clients perceived her a mere apprentice or assistant—always called upon but never compensated. They may not have realized the satisfaction she derived from her role behind the scenes. The very fact that Frank expected her to use her education to pursue a career made him, in her mind, the fairest partner she could hope for. That he showed any concern with running their home and raising their children also made him, she thought, uniquely progressive among American men. Lillian would always be the more consistent parent, but Frank's unusual interest in domestic affairs caused her to see him as a more involved parent than he likely was. She described her marriage as a "fifty-fifty"[2] arrangement, each contributing his or her strengths to the maintenance of the whole.

Lillian spent most of her first year in marriage on field trips to construction sites, learning the ropes. A memorable visit to Rochester, New

York, brought her together for the first time with a rare woman engineer by the name of Kate Gleason. Lillian had never met a woman like her—an unmarried middle-aged construction expert, who thought it perfectly appropriate to climb up the side of a steam engine to drive it and to not bother with traditional feminine clothing on construction sites. Lillian, too, eventually left high heels and corsets at home. Before long, she was doing the unthinkable, carrying out her apprenticeship on ladders and scaffolds, clearly pregnant, and in full view of the men on the site.

Lillian's early introduction to Gleason may have provided a false sense of opportunity to a woman beginning an engineering career, for in any subfield—mechanical, electrical, industrial, or civic—there were few other success stories from which to draw much inspiration. Gleason herself eventually left the field prematurely, forced out in large part by gender discrimination. Her short-term success was likely attributable to the fact that she, like Lillian, had been supported and trained in a family business, having never completed her engineering degree at Cornell. Likewise, civil engineer Emily Warren Roebling had essentially taken on the family business after her father-in-law died and her husband grew ill, leaving her to direct the construction of the Brooklyn Bridge (1872–1883) by herself.

Although a handful of women had earned engineering degrees by the turn of the century—Elizabeth Bragg likely the first to obtain one from an American university (Berkeley, 1876), followed by several others at the University of Illinois—women's formal training in engineering was virtually unknown in the United States at the turn of the century, and it remains a rarity today when compared to nearly all other technological fields. Mechanical engineer Bertha Lamme, who earned an engineering degree at Ohio State in 1893, had followed in the footsteps of her brother at Westinghouse in Pittsburg, only to have her career overshadowed by her engineer husband in the end. Lamme's career essentially ended with marriage, but Lillian held out hope that in her case, marriage to Frank would have the opposite effect.[3]

That September of 1905 the first Gilbreth baby finally arrived—a blond, blue-eyed girl named Anne, after her Grandmother Moller. It's a wonder that Lillian bore so many children in the years that followed, given the pain she experienced in the months after Anne's birth. She wanted to be back on her feet quickly, but she was told to stay in bed until her bent coccyx and jaundice righted themselves. All the while little Anne demanded constant attention, a prototypical "first baby," to be sure. When Lillian was ready to wean her from the breast, baby had other plans; she nursed for fourteen months before her exhausted mother forced the issue and gave her a bottle. It was a rare instance in their marriage when Frank grew nervous for his wife, much as William Moller had after Annie delivered Lillian in 1878. There was good reason for concern, since Lillian grew exceedingly thin. Frank heeded the same advice given to William Moller and sent his wife to California. The weather was milder, and his wife would find comfort in her family and friends. Frank stayed behind to tend to his thriving business.

The convalescence did Lillian wonders. She returned to New York refreshed and in better spirits—only to turn right back around to the Bay Area unexpectedly in 1906. That April, an earthquake measuring a startling 8.3 on the Richter scale killed thousands and left many more homeless. Lillian was desperate to be back with her family, all of whom survived the quake unharmed. But the timing could not have been worse; having finally weaned baby Anne, she was now pregnant again and did not look forward to another grueling train ride across the country, nauseated and with an infant in tow. Frank urged that she make the trip anyway, for he couldn't help but see an opportunity for profit in all the wreckage. Whole neighborhoods had been razed, and historic landmarks suffered such structural damage that they needed to be rebuilt from the ground up. Their hasty return to Oakland could be the difference in beating out competitors for building contracts, he told her. And thus Lillian reluctantly agreed to go.

Not only did Frank then convince investors to loan him money for a publicist and advertising, he even convinced Martha and Kit to make their own first trip out West following his and Lillian's arrival. Ever eager to please him, they agreed to tend to his house and to provide Lillian additional help with the baby as he pounded the pavement for contracts. Meanwhile, Lillian struggled to set boundaries, her parents ever watchful and controlling. In New York, they could do nothing to interfere with her day-to-day decisions, but in Oakland they liked to think that they had the last word. Annie insisted that all of the Gilbreths stay with them at the Moller estate, but Lillian held her ground and decided to rent a place nearby, where she could tend to her growing family with more autonomy. Against her mother's wishes, she took off to San Francisco, alone and pregnant, to look at house rentals and even declined her parents' chauffeur, preferring to take a public trolley car instead. She found a quaint Arts-and-Crafts row house on Ashbury Street, where she settled with baby Anne and waited for Martha, Kit, and new baby to arrive.

In this period of flux, Frank was nowhere to be found; he had already set off back East to acquire more capital, his plan harder to execute than he thought. His absence was conspicuous, but Lillian was growing accustomed to it. She thrived on the constant interactions with her friends and family in the meantime, making this pregnancy less traumatic than the last. Frank was not in town to see Anne's first steps or the birth of baby Mary in December of 1906, but, with three doting women in the house and grandparents nearby, neither baby lacked for attention.

Martha and Kit were helpful but also a source of growing anxiety, as they made it known that they felt out of place. Both complained bitterly about the California climate, and Kit seemed uncommonly agitated; only later did the Gilbreths discover that she suffered from a worsening condition of diabetes and that she was in desperate need of medical attention. The Bunker women wanted to return to New York, making Lillian weary as the months wore on. She was nursing a newborn and tending to a needy older baby in the wee hours of the night. Having once been charged with the overnight care of her siblings, the task was not unfamiliar, but it was exhausting nonetheless.

The California contracts did not pan out as Frank had hoped; very quickly modest jobs were seen to completion, and he moved his family back to New York in the fall of 1907. The new apartment he chose on 110th Street and Riverside Drive was larger and contained more amenities for his growing family. Kit and Martha were relieved to be back on familiar ground, but Kit never rebounded from her illness in San Francisco. During a family visit to Rhode Island that October, she died unexpectedly, leaving Martha to mourn her closest companion. Kit was thirteen years younger than the seventy-three-year-old Martha, yet the robust New England widow insisted that she could manage the household alone.

And thus, as Martha prepared meals for the family, Lillian found time daily to take the girls for strolls on the streets around their new apartment. The grittiness of the city made it nearly impossible to keep the girls as spotless as the maids had kept them in Oakland. Hauling prams up flights of stairs in and out of the building was laborious, and yet Lillian felt a sense of liberation in being able to tend to her children as she pleased, away from Annie Moller's watchful eyes. The girls' routine fell to the wayside when Lillian became pregnant again in the fall of 1907. She only walked and lifted prams as her body permitted, until little Ernestine arrived healthy in April of 1908. Not six weeks later, Lillian was off again to California, leaving Anne and Mary back in New York with Grandma Martha.

As always, Lillian went with the intention of visiting with the Mollers, but there was also something else important to do—Frank had hatched another plan: He had arranged for his wife to talk to administrators at Berkeley to reenroll her in a doctoral program—not in literature this time, but in the nascent field of industrial psychology. His insistence on this point was stunning, considering that he himself had dropped out of MIT, boasting that the university couldn't teach him anything that he couldn't learn by doing hands-on. In this way, he had followed in the footsteps of Thomas Alva Edison, the greatest innovator of his time, who held more than a thousand American patents—all without the benefit of professional degrees. Frank had modeled himself in this same entrepreneurial mold, and yet he understood that Lillian would likely have a harder time playing by similar rules. Self-making was considered noble in men but did nothing to lend legitimacy to a female engineer. She needed the added boost of academic degrees to earn respect, he convinced her, even though these were credentials that few of his colleagues had earned themselves.

Once again, Lillian wrote little about whether this plan was one she fully endorsed, but she went through with it nonetheless. She agreed that she could be a greater asset to the Gilbreth consultancy with a doctoral degree and that Berkeley was the best place to earn it, even if it was across the country from their home. Her track record at the university had been excellent, and, despite President Wheeler's general stance on women's education, several women had earned Berkeley PhDs by the time Lillian sought one in 1908. Taking advantage of her doting mother and sisters in Oakland, she was able to hand off baby Ernestine as she spoke with administrators and worked on drafts of *Bricklaying System*, a book she edited for Frank. The goal was to return to the East Coast with a manuscript ready to publish under Frank's name and a proposed plan of action for completing her doctoral degree.

Although Berkeley did not have an established program in industrial psychology, administrators allowed Lillian to convene a doctoral committee that included her old mentors Charles Gayley and George Stratton, as well as Jessica Peixotto, the second of Berkeley's women doctorates, who had been hired on as a faculty member in 1904. Admittedly, there were complications that needed to be smoothed out, since no one on her committee had relevant expertise in her field. There was also the undetermined decision of where she would pursue her field research. Berkeley required graduate students to spend a year in residence, but there was really no way for her to take courses or pursue research on campus, given that most of her learning and research would occur at industrial sites. She requested that her residence requirement be waived so that she could run experiments in the Northeast, in the facilities of the Gilbreths' clients. Assuming that all had been approved, Frank even hired a German nursemaid to help Martha with the children at home, freeing Lillian to observe work processes at plants around New York.

Already the pattern of working and mothering that became commonplace over the next dozen years started to come into view: Martha took care of the older children, allowing Lillian to focus intensely on her most recent newborn and the responsibilities Frank assigned her as his second-in-command. She tended to all client calls and edited the manuscripts Frank wrote out longhand on steamers and trains; with Martha at home, Lillian was able to do much of this work as she, too, traveled to clients and family members on the West Coast. Unbeknownst to colleagues, she was also the researcher of the Gilbreth pair, culling the materials to go into Frank's speeches at universities and technical meetings or for pitches he made to clients. She had become a multitasker in the modern sense of the term.

If her schedule seemed frenzied in Frank's absence, Lillian did not appear overwhelmed. In fact, she always thought it easiest to stick to a routine when he was out of town, since he was too much of a distraction when he was home. When he returned from trips, Frank burst into the house like a whirlwind, and, almost immediately after kisses and hugs, he sat down with Lillian and read off lists of new tasks he had thought up during his hours in transit. In return, his wife provided briefings that outlined engineering projects or developments that she had read about in the newspapers or technical literature. He asked for progress reports on her writing and editing, and he put her on schedules if she was not making her deadlines.

Lillian's letters back and forth with Frank from his various business meetings serve as remarkable windows into her multifaceted consciousness as mother and wife, professional and engineer during her years of early child rearing. She discussed the problems of clients as well as the children's birthdays and milestones Frank was missing on the road. His letters back expressed affection, but they were also filled with lists of urgent orders: "I'll begin by planning your work so that you can do it with less fatigue and in less time," he prefaced in a letter to his wife from Germany and then gave instructions for all his files and correspondence. Finally he reached "Item #16": "Take a *real* vacation before doing anything. You need it badly."[4] Such reminders were typical in his letters but never at the top of his lists. And yet somehow these small gestures of appreciation were enough to motivate Lillian to proceed as planned.

That she accommodated his rigorous demands suggests that Lillian felt fulfillment in playing a part in Frank's vision. Whether that vision was his alone or one she coauthored behind the scenes isn't known. In later years her children seemed to think that Mom had little to no agency in Dad's agenda. "If [Dad's] interests had been in basket weaving or phrenology, [Mom] would have followed him just as readily," Frank Jr. and Ernestine decided, but Lillian's reasons for adhering to his rigorous schedules and ambitious plans are likely multifaceted—attributable to her concealed ambition as much as to any convention to honor and obey.[5]

4

Scientific Management and the Human Element in the Progressive Age, 1909–1911

Frank increased Lillian's responsibilities in his business at just the time in her reproductive life when experts thought rest and relaxation were crucial. Medical men had long cautioned that women engaged in intellectual pursuits were at grave risk to their reproductive health, although the perpetual illnesses of Lillian's own mother seemed to confirm the converse supposition: that bearing children tapped the female body of reserves needed to do other things. But Lillian's generation was beginning to test these time-honored theories about women bodies. Although middle-class men of previous generations might have sent their wives off to spa cures for rehabilitation after giving birth to a child, Frank gave Lillian to-do lists to pass the time. She didn't quibble, since correcting the galleys for his upcoming books seemed to pass the time better than anything else after birthing a baby. Paradoxically, she found her forced convalescences to be productive and restful at once.

Although Lillian did not believe that intellectual or physical work damaged her body, others were still not fully convinced. There were poorer women on farms and in the nation's industrial plants who, to be sure, taxed their bodies to a much greater extent, and municipal reformers believed that women in factories needed protection. They celebrated the decision in the landmark Supreme Court case of *Muller v. Oregon* (1908), which limited women's work hours to no more than ten per day in order to protect their reproduction. Implicitly, this decision reinforced the notion that women could not withstand the same physical rigor as men for whom no work limitations were in place. Some workingwomen approved, much as they approved of the efforts of the National Child Labor Committee (est. 1904) to pass laws against child labor at the state level. They appreciated any measure that safeguarded exploited workers who could not protect themselves. On the other hand, such legislation put workingwomen at great disadvantage, because they were already underpaid compared to men and now their limited hours affected their earning potential even more. In Lillian's case, excessive work satisfied her restless mind; for poorer women, it fed their families and put roofs over their heads, whether they liked the work or not.

Such protective legislation was indicative of some of the measures championed by well-intentioned, if not always well-reasoned, Protestant, middle-class reformers of the Progressive Era (1880–1920). Recognizing the social ills that came with growing disparities of wealth in the industrial world, some of them tried to clean up municipal streets, others to build parks and playgrounds for the urban poor. There was never a singular ideology underpinning the Progressive Movement in America, and many "Progressives" disagreed on how best to carry out their social mission. Some, for example, favored the vote and protective legislation for American women; others thought them detrimental. Nevertheless, one finds similarities in sensibility among them. Progressives tended to believe in the benevolence of science, if properly applied and not left in the hands of a plutocratic few. Modern efficiency and social planning, the kind to which the Gilbreths claimed to devote themselves, could indeed be forces of positive social change, most believed, if conceived and executed with the right intentions. Progressives generally distrusted the corporate monopolies that had come into power in the economic climate after the Civil War, and thus they tried to keep corporations' ability to exploit and dominate in check.

Progressives had their fingers in many pies: education, housing, and nutritional, industrial, and municipal reform. The photographic journalist Jacob Riis, for example, had awakened middle-class Americans like the Gilbreths to the deplorable conditions of the urban poor through his exposé, *How the Other Half Lives: Studies Among the Tenements of New York* (1890). Riis argued that the stifling conditions of immigrant housing created tuberculosis and other diseases that added to immigrants' "depravity," or, in the eyes of moral reformers, their "fall from grace," and he successfully convinced New York legislators to pass the Tenement House Act of 1901, which banned the building of poorly ventilated tenements. Buildings were now required to have indoor toilets, open courtyards, fire safeguards, and outward facing windows—at least in theory—for the law was not always enforced.

But whatever the work of reformers during this booming industrial age, it was not nearly enough. Most corporate profits went into the hands of a small elite—factory owners and the white-collar professional class—almost always at the expense of the working poor, made up typically of immigrants from Asia and southern and eastern Europe. Add to their numbers more and more African Americans coming to northern industrial centers from the rural South, and the nation's cities bred social tension, as increasing numbers of people competed for menial, low-paying jobs.

It is not clear whether Lillian and Frank believed that immigrant laborers and workers of color had themselves partially to blame for their depravity. The Gilbreths had come from the same Anglo and Germanic stock of most robber barons and magnates of this the Gilded Age,[1] and to large degree, these "winners" in the capitalist enterprise believed that they had their own Protestant morality, work ethic, and racial makeup to thank for their success. Sometimes, consciously or not, Frank endorsed social application to British evolutionist Charles Darwin's biological law of "survival of the fittest." When theorizing about maintaining the United States' supremacy in the world, he sounded much like a eugenicist—someone who believed that the Anglo-Saxon race was more "fit" to lead than others. Most eugenicists thus inferred that no effort should be made to help immigrants and blacks rise up the social ladder, since their lowly station was as nature intended, but the Gilbreths were ambiguous on this point. No doubt Lillian's birthing of white babies was a form of "positive eugenics" in Frank's mind; rather than eliminate the "unfit," he thought it patriotic to birth more and more babies of superior stock. Though the Gilbreths sympathized with the plight of industrial workers, it is not clear that they believed industrial workers could be their mental or moral equals.[2]

If the Gilbreths had ethnically and racially biased views, they did not differ from many other Progressive reformers. That said, Lillian was not so much a Progressive in name as in spirit. Unlike single women and settlement workers like Jane Addams in Chicago and Mary Simkhovitch in Greenwich Village, she was too busy with work and raising her own children to get involved in the building of schools, health clinics, playgrounds, better housing, and rooftop gardens for the poor. By no means was she a social activist in the same direct ways as union leader Mother Jones and anarchist Emma Goldman, women who suffered arrests and bodily harm in their efforts for industrial workers. Lillian did not participate in strikes or the Socialist Party, but she did believe that the Gilbreths' designs of work processes in industrial plants were more humane than those of the other scientific managers with whom they identified after 1906. Frank, and Lillian to a greater extent, adhered to some Progressive notions about *environment* and its role in shaping the individual; she drew out this facet of their work and made it their hallmark to a large degree.

It was not just one's work environment that mattered; in Lillian's eyes the home environment, too, was a factor in raising upstanding, productive citizens. Although the Gilbreths didn't suffer the conditions of the unregulated factory or overpopulated tenement, they listened to municipal reformers who cautioned against raising children in the dirty air of the city, seeking a place where their children could run, swim, and play in the fresh air of the great outdoors. Physical exercise had not been an emphasis in Lillian's upbringing, but she thought it cruel to deny her daughters the physical training she would have sought out for sons. Both to her benefit and exhaustion, Frank, too, rejected Victorian theories about raising daughters. He had not grown up with women like Annie Moller, the image of feminine delicacy. His mother was vigorous, and his sisters were his academic superiors. He watched them cultivate their talents and bodies outside the home and swore that his wife and female children would be similarly inclined. Thus by 1909, he and Lillian agreed that the time had come to move to the more open suburbs. The decision was hastened along by news that Lillian was pregnant with their fourth child.

The Gilbreths hoped to find a house with a yard in the New York environs but also one large enough to separate infants from older children, as Lillian recalled her own sleepless nights in a house of fussy babies. More important, they needed a space that could be turned into an office to allow for the more efficient running of the family business. They found what they were looking for in Plainfield, New Jersey, but Frank could not be in town for the move, leaving Lillian once again to manage a major upheaval without him. In September she packed up the children and installed her family in its new home, all in her third trimester of pregnancy. Lillian expected the baby to come sooner than she did that November, given the timing of all her others. That fall she grew so impatient that she recruited the nursemaid to walk her around the neighborhood until she finally felt the urge to push. She named her redheaded, blue-eyed newborn Martha, and Grandma was only too pleased. In Frank's frequent absences, she had become her daughter-in-law's closest companion and greatest support. Lillian recognized that she could not take the time she did to work, study, and tutor the children had Martha not been in the home managing everything else.

The advantages of suburban life became quickly apparent to Grandma Martha as she built a rapport with the other homemakers in the neighborhood. Lillian enjoyed feeding the baby in a high chair on the porch, where she could take in the fresh air and greet neighbors walking by, though she sensed at times that they had made their judgments of her. As a woman working for a family business, she was still a relatively rare breed to whom other homemakers could barely relate. Several likely scoffed at her bearing children only to leave them behind for meetings and worksites around the city, and thus Lillian conceded that it was hard to "make much progress in women's social affairs" in Plainfield.[3] On the other hand, she felt a tinge of sanctimony towards her neighbors. She was too busy making a splash in the construction business to play bridge or make the standard social calls. And now, she had to find yet more time to research and write her doctoral dissertation.

In Frank's mind there was no time to waste, for he was progressively fashioning himself as a white-collar industrial consultant rather than a blue-collar builder, and Lillian, he decided, was the key to his reinvention. He had been thinking more theoretically about efficiency for some time, inspired by industrial engineer Frederick Winslow Taylor, a man twelve years his senior, who, by 1900, was considered the greatest innovator in American industry. Taylor had moved up the ranks to become the chief engineer at the Midvale Steel Company in the 1880s, perfecting his ideas in its production plant as he went. Developing steel tools that cut twice as quickly as others, he had patented his ideas, grew rich, and formally retired at the age of thirty-seven. Frank hadn't achieved Taylor's financial success, but he liked to think that they were cut from the same cloth: disciplined, innovative, and self-made. He was convinced that a highly credentialed wife would help him make the case.

Frank had read Taylor's seminal work "Shop Management" in 1903 and thought it a revelation. It introduced principles of "Scientific Management," the theory of analyzing and synthesizing industrial workflow for the purpose of improving labor productivity and overall economic efficiency. Taylor knew only too well about what he wrote, for at Midvale he had snuffed out all loafing with his infamous series of "time studies," which determined wages and expected rates of worker production. His rates of efficiency had been derived using a stopwatch, an instrument he believed more empirically accurate (and hence "scientific") than any form of mere human observation. Workers who finished tasks in the time the stopwatch allotted were not penalized and in theory even rewarded with time off or better pay if they were especially efficient. Taylor claimed that such a system created a win-win situation: industrial owners enjoyed lower production costs, while the speedier workers were better compensated. His emphasis on making efficient business of *management*—reorganizing administration while streamlining the processes of taking inventory, scheduling, and cost accounting— was also Frank's over time. He believed that the theory of management was the intellectual niche of the future.

"Shop Management" became the proverbial bible of the American efficiency movement, and Taylor was dubbed "the Father of Scientific Management." In fact, people often simply referred to Scientific Management as Taylorism. Taylor's election as president of the prestigious American Society of Mechanical Engineers (ASME) in 1906 was only affirmation that Frank needed an in with the renowned man, and he found one when he was introduced to Taylor in the lobby of the engineering society's building in New York that year. Taylor was gracious and paid Frank the ultimate compliment when he told him that he knew of his work and had even used an illustration of his Portable Gravity Mixer in his "Treatise on Concrete." That Taylor did not acknowledge Frank as the inventor in his text was of no concern, for this father of Scientific Management seemed willing to bring Frank into his inner circle and to share some of the work he had contracted. Frank humbly invited Taylor to his offices to show him more of his bricklaying studies, and Taylor reciprocated with an invitation to Pennsylvania to witness his latest installment of processes at the Tabor Manufacturing Company. Frank ingratiated himself even further by convening a small group of men at the New York Athletic Club to inaugurate the Taylor Society, the purpose of which was to propagate Scientific Management in American industry.

Frank's decision to move his family to Plainfield was partly to put him in closer proximity to other scientific managers like Henry Gantt, whose management charts were used to build the Hoover Dam, and Calvin Rice, secretary of the ASME. He joined up with these men and others at a joint meeting of the ASME and its English counterpart organization in 1909; this time, however, he asked Lillian to join him at the sessions in England. Baby Martha was only seven months old, but Lillian agreed that her graduate status and research were an asset. Although other wives accompanied their husbands to England for the event, Lillian was the only one to forego the ladies' receptions to take notes at the technical sessions. People approached Frank, asking if it were true that his wife had become a "business partner" of sorts. Once he would have quashed the rumors, but now he let Lillian respond to them herself.

Her responses affirmed that she was in fact abreast of Frank's work, but she typically understated her involvement. Although she made her appearances when asked, she never forgot that her most important role remained behind the scenes and that it should look that way. In a field dominated by men, her presence at meetings was politely tolerated because she did not appear to be in charge. As much as Frank wanted his wife to earn her doctoral degree, her professional reputation was always secondary to his. She understood this implicitly; it's why she took time out from her research to index a new edition of *Field System* (1908) and why she quietly did the lion's share of the preparation of manuscripts and papers for Frank's academic and professional meetings. The books *Concrete System* (1908), *Bricklaying System* (1909), and *Motion Study* (1911) were published in Frank's name only, but in truth, Lillian had worked so closely with Frank on these texts that even he could not tease out his contributions from hers. They stayed up late into the night laying out drawings and galley sheets, often handing off babies as they worked. "I never had so much fun as I have planning these things with you," he told her. "You are always such an inspiration and always go me one better on all my ideas."[4] Although others did not see Lillian as Frank's partner, his private acknowledgements seemed to be enough to sustain her.

Truthfully, Lillian also did much of the writing because she was simply better at it. Though Frank described her prose as "gabby" compared to his, he knew that hers was more inspired. Lillian underplayed her literary talent, perhaps in an effort to soothe Frank's feelings of inadequacy about his lack of formal education. Although he seemed to wear his self-taught status as a badge of honor, she understood that he was also compensating for having no college degree. To his credit, he channeled these feelings into the productive encouragement of his wife. He could see that her abilities to communicate elegantly and to think unconventionally were assets, and this confirmed the hunches he'd had ever since he first asked her to edit his works and study the goings-on at his construction sites. Frank also observed other ways that Lillian forged her own path. He would tell her what to look for to ensure that the work was being done efficiently, and yet out of the corner of his eye he could see that she focused on altogether different details: as the contractors watched the stone and Frank watched the masons' motions, for instance, Lillian stood watching the masons' faces, trying to decide if they truly liked the work. In her studious reserve and feminine upbringing, she had become observant of people and instinctive about what made them tick. This aspect of her work would determine the direction of Frank's consulting business and her own career as an engineer.

Lillian's unique perspective on work eventually created tensions between Frank and Frederick Winslow Taylor. Her objections to Taylor's methods always came down to his lack of accounting for the "human element" in industrial processes. Yes, he had streamlined industrial systems, she agreed, but only because he had removed human contingency from them. Where he could mechanize human work, he did; and when he couldn't remove human beings from his assembly lines completely, he found a way to dehumanize men in the name of science. Once workers had been skilled artisans, masters of their domains; but Taylor made them interchangeable, with no power to defend their turf. Workers were transformed into smaller and smaller cogs of a bigger industrial machine: he called the process specialization and insisted that it was progress.

Lillian reminded Frank that Taylor's system of rates turned out in practice to punish more often than reward. At the Bethlehem Steel Company, for instance, the "fair" rate Taylor established to load pig-iron was two and a half times faster than the former average and a rate that seven out of eight workers failed to maintain. Across the country, managers took his lead and instituted "speed-ups" in production: "Make *x* more shirtwaists, or table legs, or automobiles in an hour or don't get paid." Indeed the most efficacious thing a manager could do, Taylor advised, was to subscribe to the Darwinist logic of the day and simply let the weak links go.

Industrialists were quick to give social application to the theory of survival of the fittest. By 1900 many of their workers were no longer the German or Irish immigrants who had come to America earlier in the nineteenth century, but Asians or southern and eastern Europeans, unaccustomed to the Protestant ways of their employers. The cultural dissonance between laborers and management made it easier for the latter to attribute blame to the former for their own loss of marketable skills and impoverishment. It wasn't management's own greed and laissez-faire economic policies that widened the rich-poor gap in American cities, industrialists alleged, it was the workers' inherent inability to compete in a capitalist world.

Taylor paid lip service to incentives and rewards for workers, but, more than anything else, he designed management systems to keep their degenerate tendencies in check. His worldview was ultimately a pessimistic one when it came to the natural proclivities of the industrial workforce: he believed that if left to their own devices, workers would exert the least amount of energy for the greatest monetary reward. Such presumptions about hedonism coincided with those of most academic psychologists of the time, who presumed that humans were ruled by sets of universal instincts, accounting little for individual variation in their motivations or ability to learn. And thus Taylor's goal was not to make work fulfilling in any intellectual or emotional sense, just efficient. He likened industrial workers to mindless animals and designed their tasks accordingly.

Successful magnates of the day—men like Andrew Carnegie and J. P. Morgan—made their fortunes by heeding Taylor's advice. They encouraged the government to do little to mandate minimum wages and hours, employment insurance, or generally more healthful conditions in the places where their workers produced. They naturally liked the checks Taylor built into his systems more than they liked his theoretical incentives for employees. Should it be their prerogative to reward workers with extra pay and time off, they reasoned, when they could easily replace them with men more desperate for those jobs? Taylor's solution oftentimes was to keep the owners happier than workers, since they paid his fees. He was complicit in their refusal to spend money on welfare measures for laborers and assured them that their frugality was just as well. Pension plans and sanitary restrooms cut into profits, he told them. Government regulation of any kind was a disruption of free market forces, which, he contended, could naturally regulate themselves.

American workers had begun to counter the exploitative practices of American corporations as early as the 1860s by establishing unions to defend their interests. Railroad brotherhoods had sprung up in the effort to control work conditions and to institute benefits for railroad workers, and the Knights of Labor (1869) represented workers more generally in the years after the Civil War. In 1881 the Organization of Federal Trades and Labor Unions under Samuel Gompers championed the eight-hour workday in American factories. Five years later it merged with the

Knights to create the American Federation of Labor (AFL), a national organization made up largely of skilled workers. Some workers radicalized further under Socialist and anarchist banners, becoming Marxists or joining the ranks of the International Workers of the World (IWW). Between 1890 and 1914, organized labor was a force formidable enough to shorten the average workweek of industrial employees from 54.4 to 48.8 hours, but their gains in hourly wages were won for largely *skilled* workers, who most often were native white men. Women, immigrants, and unskilled workers continued to be as badly exploited as ever.

Unionists believed that many capitalist forces contributed to the widening gap in wealth between industrial owners and workers, not the least of which was Taylorism. As the clock increasingly ruled the lives of workers, rigidifying the bounds of work and leisure, they could see that a worker's quality of life was compromised. Socialist critics who subscribed to the ideas of Marx and Engels believed that no matter how a scientific manager configured the work, the effort to make it more efficient would always make profit for owners at the workers' expense. Scientific Management was not social progress, they insisted, but, by definition, a mechanism of suffering and social strife. Thorstein Veblen, sociologist and author of *The Theory of the Leisure Class* (1899), also questioned whether Taylor's well-reasoned systems of management were just cloaked forms of exploitation. In 1906 the Socialist journalist Upton Sinclair was perhaps most successful in popularizing criticism against Taylor-like efficiency when he published his novel *The Jungle*, an exposé of the horrific working conditions in the Chicago meatpacking industry, all in the name of maximizing profits.

Tensions between industrialists and labor came to a head in 1911, just as Lillian Gilbreth was starting to weigh in on the problem in a voice distinct from Frank's. At the Triangle Shirtwaist Factory in the garment district of Manhattan, 146 women and girls, largely young Jewish and Italian immigrants, died when fire broke out on the ninth floor of the worksite. In the interest of increasing productivity, needle workers had been locked into the workroom, unable to avoid the smoke and flames that engulfed them. Several who did escape the flames died anyway, suffering injuries when they jumped out of factory windows and into elevator shafts in an attempt to escape. As the Triangle employees suffered the worst effects of unchecked management, workers at the Watertown Arsenal near Boston protested their workplace becoming the next testing ground for Taylor's ideas, causing a subcommittee of the House Labor Committee to summon Taylor to a hearing. The committee decided that Taylor's systems were not only unscientific but also inhumane and banned his stopwatch from government projects.

Lillian observed all these developments in 1911 and worried that much damage had already been done. While legislators assessed the collective toll of the efficiency movement, she worried about its effects on the individual worker. How did Taylor's dehumanized methods impact a man's production, his morale, his manhood, and his sense of self in the longer term? she wondered. Only later in her career did she focus more intently on the physical, emotional, and intellectual needs of women workers; in 1911, Frank's clients had yet to employ very many of them.

Ever since studying with Thorndike, Lillian had been developing her own theories about worker behavior. In some ways she had fallen in line with theorists like Karl Marx and Friedrich Engels, men who insisted that, at the base level, human beings were driven to work because they were driven to create. Also influential to her thinking on worker motivation was the Harvard philosopher William James, who believed that each human being possessed a unique combination of aptitudes that had greater bearing on the individual's work than seeking pleasure or avoiding pain. Lillian agreed and believed that, from a psychological point of view, the very purpose of work was to express individuality. She supposed differences between individuals to be the result of learned responses to stimuli rather than of instinct. Environments shaped human beings, she contended, and human beings derived satisfaction uniquely, their means of satisfaction changing as they acquired new skills. An industrial manager could gain a worker's trust by keeping wages fair, she argued, but also by supplying him with work that was psychologically stimulating. Thus inefficiency did not necessarily lie in a worker's lack of ability; it could be the product of a manager's inability to motivate and teach. With proper instruction, she believed that workers could acquire new habits adapted to their strengths.[5]

Lillian tried to convince Frank that a focus on worker psychology would distinguish the Gilbreths from the rest of the Taylor flock, and eventually he agreed. Although he had long accounted for workers' physiology, their physical abilities, and their comfort in performing tasks, his wife's emphasis also soon found its way into publications in his name. In *Motion Study* (1911), for example, he focused on a worker's physiology as well as his "temperament" and "contentment" in the factory. A worker needed adequate tools, pleasing surroundings, entertainment, and a clear understanding of the systems of reward and punishment, he maintained, much as Lillian had in her dissertation. In *Field System*, Frank (and Lillian to an undetermined extent) told managers to cater to workers' needs with "suggestion boxes" and periodicals that stimulated their minds. The workers in the Gilbreth publications were defined more broadly than in any Scientific Management literature to date: They were factory hands, office workers, schoolteachers, homemakers, farmers, and store clerks. All of them, according to the Gilbreths, sought and deserved work that made them feel fulfilled, however they defined fulfillment.

Frank undoubtedly respected the perspective his wife brought to his field, but he also worried that it would place her at odds with other Taylorites, who valued the empirical measurement of productivity over seemingly subjective forms of gauging a worker's morale. Lillian's preoccupation with the worker's psyche could seem, in their eyes, to be an overly sentimental show of sympathy, not science. Taylor's disciples had relied on the irrefutability of empirical measurements of time and profits, and yet Lillian surmised that unquantifiable emotions of individuals also affected their bottom lines. In her hands, Scientific Management was as much process as end product, art as much as science.

In the emerging pages of her dissertation, Lillian anticipated her critics, insisting that the study of the mind was not only appropriate in the training of teachers and philosophers but also of engineers, since the efficiency of systems ultimately relied on the human beings who put them in motion. One must modify equipment, methods, and materials to make the most out of the individual worker, she explained, whose mind "is a controlling factor in his efficiency." While scientific managers "Taylorized" work, Lillian instead wanted to "tailor" it to fit each worker like a glove. Tasks should be specially incentivized, too, to accommodate individual needs and wants. Her means were humane, but she insisted that her results, too, were those desired by scientific managers. Extemporaneous movements were eliminated on the production line, as workers increased output at lower cost to their employers. Moreover, the benefits felt were shared among owners, managers, and workers in her vision; the worker received higher wages as a result of higher profits and also gained the psychological benefit of greater self-esteem as his unskilled labor grew more efficient and skilled and he became more productive. The gap between the apprenticed worker and the college-trained one would diminish, she predicted, as the relationship between labor and capital turned cooperative. The result, if all went according to plan, was industrial peace—a true win-win situation for everyone involved.[6]

Frank saw his wife's research as a necessary innovation to Scientific Management, and yet, for the sake of his reputation, he still defended Taylor like no one else in 1911. He believed that Taylor's systems needed tweaking here and there but that scientific principles and humane ends were fundamentally compatible. Thus at a gathering at the University of Chicago he suffered the wrath of protestors, including the vocal anarchist Emma Goldman, to insist that Scientific Management could benefit workers if purely conceived and properly installed. When labor leaders attacked Taylor's *Principles of Scientific Management*, Frank responded by agreeing to write *A Primer on Scientific Management* (1912),[7] countering claims that Taylor's systems were inherently antilabor. Lillian helped him to write the piece, but the book was published in Frank's name only. It was just as well; Lillian's focus was not ingratiation to Taylor but marrying industrial engineering with academic psychology. No one else was more determined to address the seeming contradiction in standardizing and particularizing human work at once. Her merging of these endeavors constituted the rudiments of the burgeoning field of industrial psychology.

In October of 1911, it appeared that some scientific managers had taken notice of her innovative thinking, for she was invited to join Frank at the first Conference on Scientific Management at the Tuck School of Dartmouth College. Lillian was both excited and anxious. Only months before, in March, she had had her first son, whom the Gilbreths named Frank Jr. Frank Sr. could not hide his elation, sending out telegrams and passing out cigars as if his fifth child were his first. As he carried on, Lillian scrambled to take advantage of the two-week "unavoidable delay" after Frank Jr.'s birth, checking galleys for their latest publications so that she could leave for the conference relatively unburdened.

Of the three hundred people in attendance at Dartmouth, Lillian had been one of thirteen women and likely the only one there in a capacity other than companion to an attendee. The sessions had promised to be packed with the nation's top efficiency experts, making Lillian eager as ever to circulate among them, but her nursing infant forced her to keep a low profile. She remained a relatively inconspicuous presence until the final day of the conference, when the chairman Morris Cooke asked her to be one of the final speakers to close out the session: "We have all been watching the quiet work of one individual who has been working along lines apparently absolutely different from those being followed by another worker in the scientific management field," he announced and then prompted Lillian to the podium.[8]

Frank was more than happy to let his wife speak on their behalf; it was her chance to tell the nation's most prominent efficiency experts all about the Gilbreth philosophy of work. In impromptu fashion, she talked about the human element and the need for bringing the study of *human psychology* to bear on systems of industrial efficiency. Academics must put themselves in conversation with industry to make the abolishment of exploitative practices the priority of the ivory tower as well as of managers on the shop room floor, she told her audience. "Scientific Management as laid down by Mr. Taylor conforms absolutely with psychology," she went on. The study of the human mind can help to flesh out the larger complex picture, to make the efficiency movement more scientific yet. Although she never expected it, the audience seemed receptive to what she was saying, making the Dartmouth conference her "coming out" of sorts.

Now the Gilbreth trademark was starting to come more clearly into view. Frank and Lillian sought the perfect alignment of a worker's anatomy, character traits, tools, and conditions, to make him (and soon her) least wasteful and most happy and productive in any field of endeavor. Lillian's emphasis on the worker's mind differentiated the Gilbreths from other scientific managers, while Frank's emphasis on the conservation of human *motion* over *time* also looked more humane by comparison to Taylorism. He maintained that when one reduced the movements required of a worker to perform a task, the result was not just efficiency of time but of energy, resulting in less worker fatigue. Frank defined this fatigue in physical terms, Lillian in mental and emotional ones. Their philosophies were complementary, reflecting their different strengths and perspectives on work.

There was more than just a general philosophy to the Gilbreths' system; there was also a nut-and-bolts way to proceed with their clients, whether in classrooms, kitchens, or industrial plants. Specifically, they reduced all tasks to basic elements called "therbligs" (nearly Gilbreth spelled backwards). Whether laying a brick or typing a memo, all workers engaged in some sequence of the therbligs *searching, finding, selecting, grasping, positioning, assembling, using, disassembling, inspecting, transporting, loading, prepositioning, releasing, transporting, waiting, resting,* and/or *planning.* By reducing the number of therbligs in a process, the Gilbreths reduced the motions and necessarily the time and physical, emotional, and material resources required to complete a task.

And thus while Taylor collected data with a stopwatch, the Gilbreths relied on visual images in the form of micromotion films and cyclegraphs. They recorded workers' movements and placed a special clock, a microchronometer, in view to indicate the expenditure of time in fractions of seconds. They marked off work spaces into four-inch squares or photographed this cross sectioning onto film so that workers' movements could be measured spatially when projected onto screens and studied under magnifying glass. From there, they transferred the data from their films onto simultaneous motion cycle (or "simo") charts that revealed when therbligs were needlessly duplicated, dispensable, or performed simultaneously by other body parts.

Drawing on recent innovations in chronophotography, the Gilbreths eventually pioneered yet another tool of motion study, the "stereochronocyclegraph." Strapping lights onto the limbs of workers and capturing on time-exposed photographs the paths of light created as workers performed their tasks, they could measure wasted motion. The shorter and more fluid the lines, the more efficient the movements. Negatives viewed through a stereopticon revealed motions in three dimensions;

and because the Gilbreths set up their cyclegraphs with an interrupter that made the lights appear to flash at a known rate per second, they could count white dots on their photographs, measure distances between them, and determine workers' speed and relative acceleration with greater precision than with a stopwatch alone. Using such techniques, the Gilbreths boasted that they had found "The One Best Way"—the least taxing method to move the fewest body parts the least space the quickest.[9]

In an attempt to reconcile her work with Taylor's, Lillian maintained that her focus on the human element and Frank's focus on motion did not compete with Taylorism so much as complement it. Nevertheless, her focus on the individual worker and Frank's doing away with the stopwatch looked so much more humane by comparison that Taylor grew defensive. Eventually, the press demonized him so badly that he launched a smear campaign of his own. During hearings in Washington, he claimed that Frank Gilbreth's study of motion had fallen under the rubric of his time studies all along—that it was merely Taylorism repackaged to suit the times. Lillian had wanted Frank to make a break from Taylor, and now Taylor had essentially forced his hand.

One biographer has described the Gilbreths from this point forward as the Martin Luthers of Scientific Management;[10] indeed what occurred can aptly be called a sort of excommunication. Rather than defend themselves as devout followers of Taylor, the Gilbreths reinvented themselves as enlightened heretics of the efficiency movement and sought converts of their own. They had their critics who called their chronocyclegraphs a gimmick, not science, but Frank and Lillian insisted that their methods achieved precision and were thus more scientific than Taylor's, in addition to being humane. Their emphasis on diminishing *fatigue* put them in the business of *conservation*, they explained, not exploitation. Motion study, as they perfected it, did not strip the worker of autonomy because it brought skill and pride to the work; in fact, participating in the micromotion films made the worker an integral member of their investigative team. Amidst unions' mounting criticism of Scientific Management's dehumanizing effects, the Gilbreths claimed to achieve sound science and to account for the human element at once.

The Gilbreths had reason to feel assertive, but Lillian worried about the psychological toll of Taylor's betrayal on her husband. She studied the needs of industrial workers over the next months and years, but she also watched her husband, trying to understand how best to motivate him, given his unique emotional makeup. There was no point in belaboring the fallout with Taylor, she decided; her husband was too proud a man to admit that he had been duped, let alone to find inspiration in that fact. Quietly, instead, she boosted his confidence by rechanneling his energies, as well as the theoretical rationales he had once used to forge his reputation as an innovator. With utmost care, she brought her feminine perspective to his work, while allowing him to feel in charge. She made him believe, once again, that everything was going according to a plan of his careful devising.

5

Dailiness in Providence, 1912–1916[1]

After witnessing his wife's warm reception at the Dartmouth Conference, Frank urged her to finish her PhD thesis and to publish it while the iron was hot. He suggested a rigorous writing schedule, and they hired stenographers to transcribe notes she spoke into a Dictaphone placed near the home office phone. Even as Lillian nursed, she now had little excuse not to be working actively toward completion of her dissertation. She merely spoke into the mouthpiece, without exerting more time and energy than she would have otherwise. In fact, she was following the practices that conformed to their same philosophy on shop room floors—efficiency without exploitation, productivity without physical exhaustion—at least in well-intentioned theory. But when Lillian finally submitted "The Psychology of Management" for the doctoral degree early in 1912, it was not the momentous occasion they had hoped. Berkeley officials decided that her required year of residence had not been waived after all, and her thesis was summarily denied.

Frank would not be deterred; now he assured Lillian that she didn't need the stamp of a university; they would find a publisher to distribute her book more broadly outside of academia, he promised, where there would be greater use for it anyway. He did not anticipate pounding the pavement for another two years, since no publisher dared to print this woman-authored work. Harvard psychologist Hugo Munsterberg, meanwhile, went on to publish *Psychology and Industrial Efficiency* (1913) to rave reviews, making Lillian's analysis of worker psychology appear less innovative than it did only two years before. Desperate to get his wife's work out in any form, Frank had parts of it published serially in *Industrial Engineering and Engineering Digest* under "L. M. Gilbreth," until Thomas Walton of Macmillan agreed to publish it in its entirety under the same gender-neutral name in 1914. The reprinting of *The Psychology of Management* three and four years later suggests that the strategy was likely the best one.

If only the rejected dissertation had been the most urgent of Lillian's problems at the close of 1911. As she was helping Frank mitigate the damage caused by Taylor's testimony in the governmental hearings in Washington, there was a more frightening development with which she had to contend at home: without any forewarning her two eldest girls, Anne and Mary, contracted diphtheria and required her constant care. Anne improved in time, but the same could not be said of Mary, who grew sicker with the passing days. Doctors thought the situation so grave that they called for the child to be quarantined from the rest of the household. Despite all efforts to save her, five-year-old Mary died in January of 1912.

Frank and Lillian could not bring themselves to plan a funeral or to speak of their daughter's death publicly, but their anguish was not lost on anyone who innocently asked thereafter how many children they had in their household. Their daughter Ernestine confided years later that her mother felt tremendous guilt. She had wanted nothing more than to hold Mary in her arms in those final days, but she painfully heeded warnings to stay away so as not to infect the other children. Lillian would be forever plagued by the belief that she could have saved her daughter if given the chance, with motherly love if nothing else.[2] This was the human contingency for which one could never plan, and it reinforced Lillian's desire to understand the human element of labor. She still saw efficiency as a noble aim, but not at the expense of an individual being's physical and emotional needs.

Indeed there were so many emotions that needed tending to in the Gilbreth home early in 1912; both parents and children wanted to leave Plainfield and the memories of what had happened there behind. Ironically, Frederick Winslow Taylor had provided an out for them, since he had earlier presented Frank with a professional opportunity that looked more attractive now, given the circumstances—a chance to direct an installation at the New England Butt Company, which produced braiding machines, in Providence, Rhode Island. Frank signed a contract with the company and the family moved to Providence in May of 1912, much to everyone's relief and approval. Transporting four young children and Grandma Martha nearly two hundred miles was not easy, but Lillian knew life would be more tranquil on the other end. Frank's sister moved from Brookline and now lived on the east side of town, near Brown University, and she offered to lend a hand once they arrived and settled in.

Frank was expected at the new site right away. Pressed for time, the Gilbreths rented a house until they could find something permanent. A professor of Greek archeology sublet his home to them while he was conducting research abroad. The arrangement was fortuitous but not ideal for this family with small children, given the breakable busts and classical figurines in all corners of the house. Frank, as always, turned the situation into a teachable moment by suggesting that Lillian lecture the children about the great Greek and Roman myths behind the art. Lillian, as always, added his request to a to-do list growing larger by the day.

The early months in Providence were unsettling, and it took a while for Lillian to adjust. She began to understand why Annie Moller had been such an anxious mother: there was nothing more worrisome than birthing a child after burying another, and yet she was already expecting again. She grew more anxious yet when two of her younger children came down with diphtheria, much as her eldest daughters had in Plainfield. Little Anne was traumatized, for no one knew how the children had been exposed and she worried once again about losing a sibling. To everyone's relief, both children recovered quickly and fully. From then on, Lillian made a concerted effort to put the illnesses of the past year behind her and to rebuild her family as if tragedy had never struck. Although Providence did not provide the hustle and bustle of New York, it was a modest base of operations where, in time, everyone came to feel comfortable, happy, and energized. She went on to conceive another six children in Providence, as she helped Frank build up the Gilbreth consultancy.

The Gilbreths eventually moved out of the rented house and into half of a large clapboard house at 71 Brown Street, less than a block away from the campus of Brown University and only blocks from Aunt Anne's house, where the children took their music lessons. One of Anne's music students introduced Lillian to a British woman named Mrs. Cunningham, who fell in readily as the family's trusted house-keeper, assisting Martha in all things domestic. She was nothing less than a stabilizing influence, as Frank and Lillian adhered to frantic travel, research, and writing schedules, matched only by the children's ever-shifting dockets of lessons and activities. Every day, no matter the circumstance, Mrs. Cunningham assumed her place in the kitchen and provided hot meals for the bodies coming and going in and out of the house. Her "companion," an Irish man named Tom Grieves, became the Gilbreths' handyman, despite Lillian's initial reservations. His rela-tionship with Mrs. Cunningham was ambiguous: perhaps he was her common-law husband, but no one was really sure. Over time the Gilbreths thought it best to simply overlook any air of impropriety, since the odd domestic arrangement suited their unorthodox needs. Over time the couple had even become a permanent fixture in the fam-ily's weekly councils, which mirrored the meetings the Gilbreths devised between management and workers at the New England Butt Company. As employees in the Gilbreth household, they voted and deliberated on household affairs as if they were Gilbreths themselves.

Martha, Mrs. Cunningham, and Mr. Grieves took care of most of the domestic tasks; all that was left was the tutoring of the children to Frank's strict specifications. Lillian found a willing candidate for the job in Helen Douglas, a student at Pembroke, the women's college of Brown University. She had no experience in pedagogy, and oddly that was what recommended her in Frank's eyes. He had such unconventional ideas about the instructional programs for his children that he thought it best to hire someone unfamiliar with the standard educational theories; the young, open-minded Douglas turned out to be ideal. Tutoring the eld-est Gilbreth girls each afternoon, she freed up Lillian to spend more time on the installation at the New England Butt Company, which grew especially time consuming from July of 1912 to August of 1913. Frank assured her that he did not always need her on company premises, so she designed at home the motion study experiments that he ran at the plant. The arrangement appealed, given Lillian's state of pregnancy for most of these months. As Helen Douglas played with the girls, Lillian worked in the home office and tried to keep off her feet.

The problems she aimed to solve for the New England Butt Company were intricate and challenging. Workers at the plant manufactured everything from hinges for doors to the braiding machines needed to make fishing lines, corsets, curtains, and military outfits. The varied nature of their product lines made it essential that each motion study process be specially tailored and custom designed. By the end of the contract, the Gilbreths could boast a reduction of movement by 75 percent in some of the processes and a definitive improvement in all of them. Along with micromotion study, they introduced one of their most innovative management devices: the "process" or "flow" chart, a precursor to modern-day flowcharts, for visual analysis of production at all its stages. They made adjustments to management practices, scheduling weekly feedback meetings in which managers and workers aired their grievances, and they also implemented a lecture series for workers and a suggestion box, accompanied by prizes for the most thoughtful of submitted ideas. The goal was to get the workers to feel as though they were participants and shapers of the changes taking place. To keep them motivated, the Gilbreths also installed their "three-point promotion plan" throughout the plant: At any one time, workers acted as students to the workers above them, as teachers to the workers below them, and as teammates to the workers at their level. In this way, they felt the satisfaction of mastery, efficiency, camaraderie, and self-betterment. Lillian was the mastermind of these psychological interventions.

The Gilbreths called what they had achieved at the New England Butt Company an artful science, but a science nonetheless, and their successes made Frank adamant as ever that Lillian get back to work on her PhD. At this stage, she was far less receptive to the idea than before. Since they had come to Providence, the Butt Company contract and the daily activities of the children kept her busy enough, she assured him. Particularly in light of the arrival of their newest addition, little William, she felt the time had come for a hiatus from her busy schedule. This baby had been born weaker than her other children, and she believed that he needed that much more time with his mother, nursing until he put on weight; never again would a child fail to thrive on her watch. The older girls too, she reminded Frank, were taking up more and more of her time, despite the hired help. Frank could not disagree, for, though his girls went to a respectable private school with progressive instructors, he objected to enough of their pedagogy to insist that Lillian supplement their lessons with tutoring at home beyond what Helen Douglas was giving them. While he was away, Lillian taught the children German, the metric system, geometry with wooden models—all knowledge and skills that their father supposed would give them an edge in international business and the technical world. Lillian did not disagree, but she reminded Frank that with all that was expected of her, she simply had no time to pursue a doctoral degree again.

But Frank rarely registered his wife's apprehensions about anything once he hatched a plan in his head. In fact, he had already been making arrangements with Brown University administrators, including the university president himself, to create a program of study for her—a doctoral degree in "applied management." Lillian's approval, in other words, was merely a formality. But Frank assured her that she would be given credit for coursework already completed, shortening the amount of time it should take for her to earn the degree. Would she have to write another dissertation from scratch, she asked? Yes, but "don't worry, Boss," Frank joked, "You can see our house from the classrooms. If you see one of our girls climbing out a window, you can run home and catch her before she hits the ground."[3]

Amidst her growing anxiety about baby William, Lillian also agreed to accompany Frank to Germany for another professional meeting. The baby would surely put on weight if Lillian took him overseas, Frank reasoned, for then William wouldn't compete with the other children for her undivided attention. The plan sounded just fine in theory, but she worried about how she would actually divide her time; ultimately William would be her responsibility much more than Frank's, making it hard for her to sit in technical sessions. Already on the trip across the Atlantic, Lillian noted that she was "too busy with him [Little Bill] to be sea-sick." Frank agreed that the baby was a handful, which was why he had cabled friends in Berlin to arrange for a baby nurse to be waiting once they arrived. Lillian was anxious about entrusting her baby to another's care, but the nursemaid proved more competent and organized than anyone she had ever met. Not only did she soothe the baby ably, she also did laundry, errands, and kept track of Lillian's appointments. Little Bill put on weight, and Lillian actually got to enjoy the meetings, the socializing, and the restful slower pace of not having to be at home.[4]

Indeed, the experience reinforced that Lillian could accomplish much with the help of others along the way. Frank, to his credit, understood that his goals for his wife would never be achieved without plenty of hired help in the house, and thus the domestic staff expanded to accommodate Lillian's increasingly frenetic schedule: in addition to Mrs. Cunningham and Tom Grieves, he added an occasional cook and governess, more maids, and a part-time laundress and hairdresser to lighten the load. Such an extensive network of help was not unusual in wealthy families, and indeed Frank's business thrived for most of their years in Providence. Given his priorities, he also likely devoted a greater proportion of income on hired help than others who hadn't a wife working and schooling at once.

In her years as a graduate student, Lillian did not make a meal or scrub a floor; the children were her only persistent "chore," so to speak, though indeed she never viewed them that way. Frank had instituted an "interruptions chart," limiting the number of times each child could come to their mother then she worked on her writing and research. Admittedly, of all Frank's systems, this was the one that Lillian enforced the least, since she hated to turn a child away; her preference was to be a hands-on mother when she could. Grandma Martha, still vigorous enough to oversee operations, was protective of Lillian's schedule, however. On weekdays, she helped her daughter-in-law maintain a strict routine: two hours for breakfast and the grooming of the children in shifts, two hours to research and write, a fifteen-minute break with the children before lunch, another hour with children, a half-hour nap, a half hour with the youngest baby, another hour writing, an hour for callers, an hour with the children, a half hour for miscellany, and an hour for dinner before putting the little ones down, helping with homework, and reading bedtime stories. Lillian insisted that the key to keeping focused was her afternoon nap: ten minutes of lying flat on her back did more to eliminate fatigue than ten hours of sleep once exhaustion set in, or so she liked to think.[5]

Frank had joked about catching children out of windows, but in fact it made all the difference that the Gilbreths' house was so close to campus. Lillian found it helpful to be able to run home between lectures to nurse the baby, often before anyone realized she was gone. The only problem was that the house at 71 Brown Street, although convenient, was too cramped to stay in for much longer. The Gilbreths needed a bigger house and jumped at the chance to buy the corner lot when it went up for sale. The efficiency systems Frank devised in Plainfield were perfected in this new house, for the whole left side of it became devoted to the family business. Whereas the storage of paperwork had been a problem, now they could keep their voluminous "Notes-File," which contained all the literature, photographs, publicity, and papers accumulated over the years. Again, Lillian watched the children and took notes almost seamlessly once Frank installed Dictaphone equipment on both the first and second floors. "If I haven't but fifteen minutes to dictate," she once explained, "I utilize that time"; eventually, she called this "the secret to the annual book."[6]

In the new house Lillian had a larger office and lab space for motion study, and the living room, too, was spacious enough to convert into a micromotion lab for one of her first experiments with women. Domestic science students from Columbia University's Teachers' College came to Providence to demonstrate the art of efficient bed making, providing data that became more significant later in Lillian's career. For now, the Scientific Management of the home remained a side interest, especially while Frank had better paying clients to tend to than homemakers. Nonetheless, it's clear in his efforts to make his wife efficient in her home that he understood the value of this work—and that he acknowledged domesticity *as* work—thus paying professionals to do it. More than ever, Lillian needed all the time they freed up for her. Amidst her doctoral courses and research, she was conducting motion studies for clients and had another baby, number seven—a girl that Frank insisted they name Lillian Jr.

Of course Frank was not in Providence for most of the baby's infancy. He insisted on attending the ASME meeting in Hamburg, Germany that year, for he believed that his triumph over Taylor would rely on his growing reputation in that part of the world. From overseas, he asked that Lillian continue to carry out his wishes to make the older children fluent in German as soon as possible. Lillian merely went on with her busy days, scheduling dance and music classes for the older children, conducting research for *Fatigue Study*, and actively serving on the PTA at the girls' school and in the local Association of Collegiate Alumni. In Frank's long absence, her only sign of cracking was that it took her two years to complete her course work at Brown; Frank was so confident in her abilities that he had given her the ambitious goal of doing it in just one.

With her system of help in place, Lillian reported to Frank that her doctorate work progressed slowly but satisfactorily throughout the months of 1914. There was no need to concern him about her minor setbacks, for she could sense in his letters from Jena and Berlin that he felt a real weight on his shoulders. He wrote of the tensions that had unfolded since the assassination of Archduke Ferdinand, the heir to the Austro-Hungarian throne, setting off the chain of events leading to World War I. As hostilities escalated he could only ponder the war's effects on his clients in particular and on systems of human production more generally, and he began to devise strategies for boosting industrial efficiency. Most innovative of them all were his plans for the rehabilitation of debilitated soldiers returning to the domestic workforce. As he explained to Lillian, he had witnessed trainloads of wounded men returning from the battlefields in Germany—"a grewsome [*sic*] sight"— exacerbated by the fact that they would likely contribute nothing to the civilian workforce if they survived their wounds.[7] It made him worry for American men when they inevitably entered the fray of war. It was only a matter of time, he told Lillian, and when it happened the Gilbreths needed to be seen as the industrial experts with a patriotic plan, both for soldiers on the battlefield and those returning to a productive life afterward.

As forward thinking as he was, Frank did not predict the extent to which Americans would mobilize for battle in the coming years. By the closing months of the Great War, almost five million Americans will have been enlisted into service of some kind, over 1.5 million troops deployed to France alone. In Lillian's written recollections, she was surprisingly silent about how she, a German American, was feeling about the mounting tensions between Axis and Allied powers in 1914 and 1915, for anti-German sentiment was beginning to find expression in the local newspapers and among acquaintances who talked ominously amongst themselves. Harvard psychologist Hugo Munsterberg, perhaps the man whose work in industrial psychology most resembled Lillian's in these years, ultimately felt that he had to make a choice and turn his loyalties to Germany, his mother country. Lillian, however, was American born and thus stayed true to her country, despite her husband's admiration of German culture and his successes with German clients. In fact, by the time anti-German sentiment reached fever pitch in America (1917–1918), Frank had already stopped traveling to Germany regularly, his German clients less profitable since money was harder to transfer across borders. When this juncture of the war approached, the Gilbreths had already proven their patriotism by writing papers on wartime industrial efficiency, often based on their experiences with German companies in 1914. Unlike other Americans with ties to Germany, their loyalty to country would never be questioned.

So much was going on overseas in the summer and fall of 1914, and yet Lillian was not yet thinking about war, too consumed with her harried daily existence in and around Brown University. Her tenth wedding anniversary came and went, but she barely noticed as she finished up the dissertation. Frank could not be stateside, but he wrote of his undying affection—and of the paper he wanted her to draft for the ASME annual meeting. He returned home briefly, long enough to speak at Clark University, where the famed sociologist G. Stanley Hall had also started to take an interest in the study of fatigue. Frank returned to Providence to talk to colleagues about motion studies in the surgery

wards of hospitals he planned to visit in Naples and Milan, which dove-
tailed nicely with his international work for the handicapped. He returned to Providence after Christmas but was already back in Europe in
early 1915; trips to Boston, the Midwest, and back to Europe again
meant that it was unlikely he would be home to lend support during his
wife's oral examination.[8]

"I hope that the thesis will not give you nervous prostration," Frank
wrote from Germany in April of 1915.[9] Lillian's dissertation deadline
and June graduation were nearly upon her, so she simply plugged along
with the research and writing in his absence, finally completing a four-
hundred-page dissertation called "Some Aspects of Eliminating Waste in
Teaching." Most of the hundreds of hours of field observation required
for it had taken place in local elementary schools to bring efficiency to
the classroom, a realm that male scientific managers had completely
ignored. She gave recommendations for optimal lighting, clothing,
ventilation, desks, supplies, and classroom layouts to economize on
physical motions, and she advised teachers on how to plan lessons in
advance. But again, the strength of the thesis was its insight into the
human element—what motivates teachers to teach and students to
learn. She described what a psychologist later coined "the Hawthorne
Effect," which was observed among workers at the Hawthorne Works
outside Chicago in the 1920s: like the workers simultaneously involved
in her micromotion studies, teachers and students proved eager to improve when they were made active partners in her experiments.[10]

For teachers, there was something validating about a researcher
studying their conventionally female work. Lillian did not know it yet,
but her research in the Providence schools was to be her first foray into
the kind of work that later defined her: She revealed the "science" in
women's teaching—and later she revealed the science in women's cooking and cleaning—thus validating women to male experts who thought
them too subjective to take seriously. Up until now, most Americans
viewed science as synonymous with objectivity, empirical methodology,
and technical expertise, which seemed antithetical to women's ways of
thinking and being. Whether it was taking care of children, the ill, or
the aged in the home or hospital or teaching children in schools,
women's work was thought to be too sentimental to be treated as scien-

tific, and in this Progressive Age science was heralded as all-authoritative. Lillian later insisted, as she did for Providence teachers in 1915, that women's sphere of influence can be made scientific and that empirical methods can improve on women's work, making it more fulfilling and efficient. By associating science with women's endeavors, she lent prestige to women both in and outside the home.

With the thesis complete, there was nothing left to do but the defense, an experience that turned out to be more harrowing than Lillian had anticipated. One of her examiners rejected her definition of human psychology from the start, making the rest of her claims difficult to defend. The examiners left the room to do their deliberating, and she was convinced that she had failed; but when they returned, they told her that she passed. Finally, she had completed all the work for the PhD. On the day of Lillian's graduation from Brown, Frank was on a steamer back to New York. Thankfully, Helen Douglas was at the ceremony to lend support. She herded the older children up to campus looking their best to watch their mother, the lone woman doctor, make her processional rounds around the campus green. In the past, Lillian had been sheepish in the spotlight. Once, sensing the torture of it, Frank had met his new wife on a subway platform shouting, "How are you? Have you got your divorce yet?" merely to watch her shrink with mortification. But now, as a woman with a doctoral degree, Lillian felt entitled to be conspicuous in ways her mother warned her never to be. She beamed at her brood of children on the green that graduation day, inviting onlookers to wonder about how she managed her motherly duties and scholarship at once. Later, when she met up with Frank on the pier in New York harbor, she was unshaken by his creating a scene. "Did you get it?" he yelled. She nodded in the affirmative.[11]

With "PhD" behind her name, it could now appear with Frank's on all their professional papers—more than fifty in total over the next nine years. And yet, oddly, her daily existence felt much the same. She nursed babies, transcribed notes, and tended to professional correspondence, often as Frank sat in hotel rooms pouring out his ideas for the future. "I'm still thinking of the paper you wrote for the Academy of Science. I think that and the Toronto paper and one or two at Dartmouth and some of the old ones printed in Industrial Engineering would make a good book for say $1.00 . . . Yes Boss, I see many books that we can put over, easily one a year the rest of our lives and perhaps two."[12]

There was not much Frank thought his wife unable to do, and her assets were not lost on other men who paid Frank the occasional compliment about his uniquely accomplished wife. Brown University president W. H. Faunce insisted that he did "not know another woman in America who has achieved what she had done in the realm of study, and at the same time fulfilled every duty of motherhood in her constantly enlarging home."[13] He did not know that the Gilbreths had quietly suffered the loss of a child following the graduation celebrations of 1915. The baby girl Lillian inconspicuously carried under her doctoral robe that June was stillborn in September; she and Frank said nothing about it, afraid that the news would cause friends and family to think that she was trying to do too much, too fast.

In Frank's mind especially, there was no time for criticism, since there was still so much to do. It was not enough to be seen as an opportunist; he dreamed of a longer, more respectable legacy, and his credentialed wife was yet again the key to his plan. Until now Frank had been an academic outsider, never benefiting from the clout associated with scholarly institutions. So why not academicize motion study, he thought? By opening an institute, he could create an aura of authority in Scientific Management and perhaps even win over generations of younger industrial managers for the long term. Perhaps over time he would even build a historical legacy to match Taylor's. Yes, the New England Butt Company would be the perfect place for managers to convene from Boston, New York, and overseas, he figured, for then students could attend lectures and watch micromotion experiments firsthand.

As Lillian had always been the one to stress pedagogy, she and Frank agreed it was only fitting that she do most of the legwork to carry out his vision. The very summer she graduated from Brown, she held the second session of the Gilbreth Summer School of Motion Study, and she ran the school for two more consecutive years. Frank helped Lillian plan the first summer of sessions, but he also maintained a heavy travel schedule despite them, fully confident that his wife could conduct classes without him. Apparently, he was right. The students the summer school attracted to Providence represented various colleges; they were so thoroughly convinced of the soundness of the Gilbreth System by the end of the summer that they vowed to start "Fatigue Elimination Days" on their respective campuses. Frank could think of no better publicity for his firm. And yet the day after the students left Providence in late August, Frank was again off overseas, perhaps leaving Lillian to ponder the obvious question: When was her own Fatigue Elimination Day ever going to come?

6

Battles on the Home Front
and War Front, 1916–1918

Frank boasted that a handkerchief manufacturer benefited so significantly from his reduction of movements on the assembly line that workers finished three times more cloth per hour with no perceptible fatigue. Secretaries of the Remington Company, meanwhile, learned to perform calisthenics to add to their flexibility, strength, and blood flow, all of which contributed to their winning the National Typewriting Championships of 1916. Surgeons, too, discovered that they could remove the therbligs "search," "find," and "select" from their operating protocols by calling out numbered instruments as nurses placed them squarely in their palms. Major league baseball teams signed up to have their batters, catchers, and pitchers filmed and analyzed, sparking the interest of football players, golfers, and track athletes also looking to improve their performances. Frank lined up work in Canada and spoke to audiences at Columbia and Yale as he consulted for the National Surety and performed motion studies on clerks working cash registers. From appointments in the American Posture League and the Simplified Spelling Board, to paid consulting work for US Rubber, Ford, Lever Brothers, Eastman Kodak, Erie Forge Steel, Filenes, Barber Asphalt, and American Radiator, Frank Gilbreth soon had his fingers in more pies than any other man in the efficiency business.

Not only did Lillian's doctoral credentials open the Gilbreths up to an expanded profile of clients, but the tides had also taken a drastic turn in efficiency circles. Frederick Winslow Taylor died suddenly of pneumonia in 1915, and traditional Scientific Management seemed to die with him. His legacy in the field had been unmatched, but there was no consensus on the net benefit of his innovations in American industry. Unionists thought them evil instruments of human exploitation. And yet, for all the backlash against his systems, there were still Progressives who believed that the *science* of the efficiency movement could be channeled toward industrial profit and social good at once. With Lillian's help, Frank vowed to become the most recognized face of this enlightened philosophy, working frantically to fill the void left by Taylor. In 1916, his strategy was to proselytize about the one thing in addition to motion study that made the Gilbreth management program so utterly distinctive: its emphasis on eliminating worker fatigue.

Few efficiency experts ever understood the degree to which this preoccupation originated with Lillian, and yet she had always been the one to stress the conservation of human energy over maximized production. Frank was wise to follow her lead, making it his standard practice to replace light bulbs and work surfaces to reduce workers' eye and muscle strain and to build rest periods into routines—all to improve productivity over the longer term. One publicity stunt, his "Fatigue Museum," was a visual display that made his philosophy understandable to any layman, woman, or child. It contained badly designed chairs, workbenches and "instruments of needless torture" to underscore the benevolence of his innovations by contrast. This emphasis on fatigue won Frank high-profile work with the National Safety Council, the Eyesight Conservation Group, and the Posture League, organizations that otherwise would have seen no use for Scientific Management.

Frank had a knack for publicity. He distributed glossy pamphlets, films, and images of his cyclegraphs of industrial workers, but also of women in the kitchen, to make clear that the Gilbreth system was far reaching, accessible, and humane. The images that likely left the most lasting impression were those depicting his family's daily life at home.

Nothing bespoke the human element better than his wife and scientific partner tending to babies and school lessons amidst America's impending involvement in the Great War. Lillian's look of domesticity appealed to traditionalists who, amidst a radicalizing suffrage movement, worried that professional work and political involvement denatured the once-maternal Victorian woman. Particularly during international crisis, much of the patriotic rhetoric directed toward women strongly urged them to stay home to protect traditional family values. To the hundreds of thousands of middle-class women who belonged to the Women's Christian Temperance Union (WCTU) and other antialcohol organizations, Lillian looked to be the ideal propagator of their patriotic and moralistic message: she was the mother who eschewed unsavory displays of degeneracy in saloons and protest movements for more wholesome domesticity.

That World War I preoccupied Americans in 1916 was a source of frustration to organized women's suffragists who had made legislative headway in recent months but still could not persuade the political parties to commit fully to their cause. Presidential candidates at both the Republican and Democratic conventions could no longer ignore the clamor of women parading in the streets for the elective franchise, though they staved off their demands for the time being. In his bid for re-election, the Democrat, President Woodrow Wilson, felt obliged to show tepid support for the suffrage cause. But he also told women to be patient, given the greater urgency of impending war overseas. Carrie Chapman Catt, president of the National American Women's Suffrage Association (NAWSA), made the tactical move of declaring her organization in favor of American intervention in the war, despite being a pacifist herself; the hope was that American women would be rewarded for their patriotism in the end, when grateful legislators finally passed women's suffrage, which they did in 1920.

Catt was slightly older than Lillian Gilbreth, but others with more radical sensibilities were younger than her—in their teens and twenties. These women, led by Alice Paul and Lucy Burns, broke with their mothers' generation of suffragists in the NAWSA to form the National Women's Party (NWP), an organization that fought for women's suffrage through a campaign of civil disobedience for a sweeping federal amendment granting the vote to all women in the country. Whereas their mothers generally sided with the temperance ranks and believed that women deserved the vote as moral influences on society, radical women eschewed such maternalist politics in favor of natural rights ideology: it was that women were the inherent equals of men that made them worthy of the vote, they insisted. And unlike their mothers, they went on hunger strikes and performed in ways unbefitting proper ladies to make their point. Radical suffragists, in other words, had departed completely from the mantra of Annie Moller, appearing in newspapers for their arrests and militant protests. The press often referred to them as "suffrage noise."

The women of the NWP were much clearer about where they stood on feminist issues than was Lillian Gilbreth. Sometimes her actions contradicted her words, and of course there was no accounting for how her views would change over time or how American women might interpret her increasingly public image. She was not an organized suffragist, nor did she call herself a feminist, but her example may have indicated other things to American women. Although she was a mother, she was also a professional woman with technical expertise that gave her authority in the masculine realms of industry and engineering. Younger women might have found something to appreciate in the images of the industrial psychologist with her children, for here was a woman who proved that duties at home need not preclude carving out other niches of achievement. Motherhood and career were not mutually exclusive choices to Lillian Gilbreth, who decided not to wait for suffrage to operate in the public sphere on her terms.

Indeed Lillian straddled two generations of women and, remarkably, appealed to both. In this, the year before American intervention in World War I, she was a mother who had a profession, a PhD, and knowledge of the world beyond the walls of her home. She was undoubtedly abreast of the goings-on in the suffrage movement, as an educated woman living around the epicenter of its activity. But she was too consumed with the work in front of her—both technical and domestic—to participate in the movement in any formal way. Through 1915 and into 1916, Frank was traveling internationally, leaving her to wrap up another semester of the Gilbreth Summer School and to check galleys for *Fatigue Study*, a book that she practically wrote alone.

Frank's absence while she drafted the book may have explained why it was a "popular" rather than "scientific" presentation of the merits of fatigue elimination, as she described it. Her accessible writing style allowed laypeople to understand the value of rest periods, comfortable seating, and stimulating literature in the workplace, for fatigue came in physical and mental forms. Frank thought the book "gabby," but others lauded it as the best written of the Gilbreth works. *Applied Motion Study*, which came out the following year, had more of Frank's distinctive style, perhaps because the chapters were technical articles they had already presented in front of audiences of engineers. Frank often seemed more interested in the volume and prestige of the Gilbreth publications than in their accessibility. Now with Lillian's dissertation behind her, it pleased him that she produced texts at a prolific rate. In these months— as in most months over the past decade—Lillian proved yet again to be productive in more ways than one: Frank was out of town when Fred, her eighth child, was born; as he would be when Dan, her ninth, was born thirteen months later.

Frank's absence belied his elation about bringing baby boys into the world, even as the sons of other parents were dying on battlefields overseas. Woodrow Wilson had maintained a stance of nonintervention in the First World War, and he continued to in 1915, even after 128 Americans perished on the *Lusitania*, a British liner sunk by German U-boats. Not until his re-election late in 1916 did his rhetoric change. German submarines continued to be hostile, and hawkish calls to arms filled the pages of American newspapers. Aware of the changing sensibilities among the American people, Wilson eventually called for war, and the Congress declared it formally in April of 1917. Frank responded much as he had in the wake of the San Francisco earthquake, prepared to turn a regrettable situation into an opportunity to expand his reach. He marketed Gilbreth and Company as the most capable of consulting firms for drawing up industrial plans during this unprecedented state of emergency.

It was a greater priority in this war than in any war before it to galvanize the component parts of the industrial complex for the purpose of national defense. President Wilson looked to open up channels of cooperation between business and science in all departments of government, and he called on engineers specifically to play a role in governmental affairs for the purpose of heightened industrial efficiency. Herbert Hoover, J. P. Morgan, Bernard Baruch, and other businessmen and engineers made it their duty to sit on the Committee on Industrial Preparedness, the Council of National Defense, or the War Industries Board. Frank Gilbreth, too, reacted as if Wilson were calling him directly to serve, and he made it his mission to become an intermediary between labor and industrial owners, both for efficiency and for the greater patriotic good.

The Gilbreths' experience on several fronts stood them well to participate in the war effort and to profit from it. Believing that the war would escalate, they had predicted that women would have to mobilize in significant numbers to work in offices and factories as men were called to battle. Thus in papers Frank and Lillian authored together, they called for more than just an uptick in defense industry production but also for a reorganization of work and a reinstatement of efficiency in all aspects of life—including in the unpaid domestic sphere. Women and children were integral to their war plans—not just because they worked in factories but also because they were the key participants in putting the home in order and making it efficient in this desperate time.

All able-bodied Americans needed to work more effectively, they insisted, but unable bodies, too, had a part to play in their management plans. The injured soldier was not useless, for the Gilbreths developed motion studies that adapted him to work environments to make him a productive contributor to the war economy and a contented worker in his civilian life. The press responded enthusiastically, calling motion study the Gilbreths' patriotic contribution to country, the key to the nation's industrial future. Still, Frank longed to play a more direct role in the war. He read of all that was going on overseas and grew listless. He wanted in on the action—if only he were young enough to enlist.

The allure of war may be difficult to appreciate today, since it is not nearly so glamorized, nor is it heralded as the cultivator of manhood as it was at the turn of the twentieth century. But this yearning burned to varying degrees in a whole generation of American men who had been untested on the battlefield. Frank's age and privileged Yankee background placed him squarely among this emasculated cohort of men who had been born after the Civil War but too long before World War I to be of enlistment age at its outbreak. Civil War veterans called the white, middle-class, educated men of this generation "overcivilized" and ill equipped not simply for the physical conditions of war but also for the hardships of strenuous modern life for which life-and-death battle prepared men. Indeed many of them had grown soft around the middle in their office jobs, and Frank Gilbreth was no exception. Commentators encouraged men of his generation to seek out tests of physical courage to harden them, and former President Theodore Roosevelt was one of them, believing that young men who engaged in rigorous athletic contests and outdoor activities would be better equipped to lead the nation in dire times. His "Rough Riders" of the Spanish-American War (1898) had been exemplars of the fit American manhood he envisioned. Toward similar ends, Walter Camp adapted the gritty game of American football from English rugby, thus turning the athletic fields of Ivy League schools into simulated battlegrounds for the purpose of molding more effective men for the modern age.

Frank Gilbreth had been too busy building his construction business in his youth to become a roughrider or football player, but he wanted to believe that his strenuous life had made him the most competent of modern men. He hadn't endured tests of physical courage to prove it, and now was his chance. During the war Walter Camp was developing national calisthenics programs for middle-aged men like Frank Gilbreth to give them this sense of virility and purpose; the volunteers for his Senior Service Corps even donned militaristic uniforms to underscore the point. But Frank wanted a more direct role in battle, and so, with no initiation on the part of the Army Corps of Engineers, he offered up his expertise in motion study to prepare American soldiers for warfare. When no one responded to telegrams, he traveled to Washington to make his case about how best to employ him for battle readiness.

Lillian appreciated that Frank had a sense of manhood to reclaim, but his midlife crisis could not have come at a worse time. Since the war, there had been an upsurge in clients, more publication deadlines to meet, and, as always, new babies to rear. Moreover, in the midst of the waiting for Frank's deployment orders, she became nurse to her children, guinea pigs for the efficiency experiment Frank referred to as the "mass tonsillectomy," so-called for its efficiency. Aside from the babies and little Martha, each child underwent the surgery in a makeshift operating room on the lower floor of the house, the upper floor serving as the recovery ward. Lillian's written recollections of the "Tonsil Party" betray little of the anxiety she likely felt as she watched her babes go under the knife. That she agreed to a plan entailing doctors performing multiple procedures under the pressure of a ticking clock speaks to her faith in Frank and medical science. Like most Americans in the early twentieth century, she did not question the truth of science or the "expertise" of men—and the handful of women—who practiced in its name as she did. Looking back, she admitted that the day of the surgeries she had "starved" with the children, likely nervous about the procedures, but she also made light of them, quipping: "Anyone who has not tried the experiment of nursing several youngsters through the convalescent period after this particular operation has missed something."[1]

Happily, the children recovered, but there was still no word of Frank's military orders. Thus in June both Gilbreths decided to attend a sociology conference in Cape Cod and to prepare for yet another session of their management summer school, this time with special emphasis on wartime concerns. Frank took his mother, now in her eighties, to Nantucket, while Lillian gathered her four girls and three boys for a trip to California to see the Mollers. Mrs. Cunningham accompanied her on the train out West, but the experience of transporting a brood of children across the continent was still nothing less than harrowing. Never before had Lillian endured that many children in cramped quarters for such an extended period of time. When the little ones grew restless, she took them to the train's drawing room, leaving Mrs. Cunningham with the others. Back and forth, back and forth she went. Never was she so relieved to finally arrive in Oakland.

It had been a long time since the Mollers experienced the chaos of young children in their home. Lillian worried that they might overstay their welcome, but her parents proved ever patient and accommodating. Naturally it took some time for the children to adjust to their environs and routines. Bill and Frank got into mischief often, and the normally placid Ernestine refused to ride in any car that was not Grandma's Packard limousine. Family friends arrived to meet Lillian's daughters, only to find them with hair bows and white dresses drenched by the backyard sprinklers. The return ride home to Providence was no less tumultuous than the ride to Oakland, on account of the excessive heat and dust on the train. Wilted from the experience, Lillian stepped foot in her house in early September feeling as though she needed a vacation from her vacation. She was exhausted, and for good reason. Days later, she gave birth to baby Daniel. *Applied Motion Study* came from the press ten days later.[2]

In all her writings about this harrowing trip out West, Lillian never so much as mentioned the strain of pregnancy, but of course she never had. Her discretion had much to do with how she had been raised. It was improper to speak publicly about being in a "family way," no matter how obvious one's pregnancy was to others. She had grown accustomed to carrying babies while tending to work, bills, writing deadlines, travel itineraries, and other children, making it nearly impossible to focus too intensely on her own physical discomforts, let alone the social expectations on pregnant women. In order to carry out all the tasks in front of her, she simply had to give herself license to operate in public space more openly than other expectant mothers, traveling, working, attending meetings, and walking in graduation processions with baby clearly on the way.

It was a mixed blessing to hear late in 1917 that Frank's persistence finally led to the military appointment he so eagerly sought. He was to report to the War College in Washington, DC, in December to be vaccinated and then Fort Sill in Oklahoma to make instructional films for soldiers learning to handle guns. His orders did not stipulate when he would be home, but Lillian promised to make do, not allowing her need for time or physical recovery get in the way of her husband's dreams of grandeur. While she nursed the baby, ran the household, and tended to the consultancy's standing clients, Frank assured her that he would be off making military history. Lillian packed his bags and began compiling material for the technical papers she presumed she'd be giving in his stead in the coming weeks.

Yet again, as Frank headed out, he made light of the Herculean tasks in front of his wife. "If you take care of the kids and answer the mail you will have [done] more than enough," he assured her. And yet almost immediately after his departure he started sending her letters with urgent to-do lists. She responded in letters back to him with assurances that she was doing everything to his specifications: she sent the motion models to the Smithsonian and the stills to colleagues, phoned the clients, sent the requested reprints, planned the "tech talk" she was giving in his absence . . . and on and on it went. She reiterated that all was well at home, though the children's interruptions were to blame for any typos in her letters to Fort Sill. She reported one January evening in 1918 that she had dashed up to the schools for parent-teacher conferences, taken Anne shopping, attended Ernestine's violin lesson, nursed the baby, put the little ones to bed, and worked in her office as she supervised the older children's homework. She moved the piano into the library and the bookshelves to the parlor, she also reported. "Now the children have a nice warm place to practise in, and I can inspect typing and piano, and work at my desk all at once."[3]

It made no sense in Lillian's harried world to cordon off family obligations here and professional ones there; she necessarily grew comfortable combining the two in a real-life efficiency experiment of her own—at least until February, when she started receiving cablegrams from Fort Sill about Frank's worsening health. At first he apparently suffered a minor bout of rheumatism, but it kept getting worse. He grew weak, and eventually he couldn't work. He was admitted to the makeshift army hospital, but his condition did not improve. The next wire to Lillian reported that he suffered from uremic poisoning, and he was even hallucinating. Doctors worried, given that the medical facility at Fort Sill was so grossly understaffed. Lillian read of Frank's deterioration and thought the situation too dire not to act. She booked a train to Oklahoma, determined to nurse her husband around the clock if she had to. She would keep vigil at his bedside, she decided, for this time doctors' orders couldn't keep her away. "If everything else failed to rally him," she would "pull him through by telling him how necessary he was," much as she had wished to do when her poor Mary stood at death's door.

She arrived at Fort Sill on March 4th, only to be told that Frank's pneumonia had set in. For weeks she stood vigil with nurses, doctors, and special consultants, wondering whether her husband would survive the hospital stay. She demanded that adrenaline be brought in from another facility to save his life if need be. Finally, what might have seemed offensive on other days was a welcome surprise: Frank came to and, quite suddenly, began barking orders to the medical staff. Relieved, Lillian told the nurses simply to heed whatever he said. This is a controlling man, she explained, his complaints were an indication that he was becoming cognizant of his surroundings and essentially feeling more like himself. By Easter he was well enough to sit up and rock on a chair on the hospital porch; within days he could put on pants and hobble around with crutches.

It looked as though the worst was now behind him, but a model patient he was not. Frank's rheumatism left him in great pain, and everyone knew it. He was frustrated that he was not regaining his strength quickly enough, and he complained relentlessly about the incompetence and inefficiency around him. Desperate to be useful, Lillian could think of nothing else to do but to echo his complaints and to keep a medical log to supplement the doctor's notes. Her entry for April 3rd provides a glimpse of what she contended with during Frank's convalescence that spring:

> Patient had hallucinations which are more or less logical. Hallucinations all have to do with experiences of "School of Fire." Worried greatly over apparent disagreement as to facts. Never varies from his usual standards. Demands cleanliness of person, consideration for others, et cetera. Prefers male attendants. Knows what is comfortable and how he can be made comfortable. Hates to be argued with. Detects lies or insincerity at once. Much disturbed by not being able to locate himself in time and space. Wants continually to know points of

the compass; which floor he is on; which side of the room; number of bed; et cetera. Allows no discrepancy in statements of others.[4]

The medical staff could only marvel at the thought that Lillian had kowtowed to the fussy demands of this man for years. Everything Frank ate in that makeshift hospital had to be prepared where he could see it, and he insisted on having a shave and sponge bath daily so that he presented himself to the world properly groomed. He didn't want to be talked down to but rather treated as the professional man that he was.

Lillian told the medical staff not to quibble with him. Speak to him like a colleague, not a patient, she told them. She protected his masculine sense of dominion ardently, knowing full well that his enlistment had, on some level, been tied to its gradual erosion of late. He had been fostering her professional and academic development, even revamping his consultancy to reflect her feminine influence. But his military tour of duty, the one thing he wanted and needed to do without her, had ended abruptly in failure. Lillian inherently understood that his manhood had been bruised. And thus when he barked complaints about a nurse's ministrations, she promptly had the nurse removed, far more assertive for her husband than she ever would have been for herself.

Frank was put off by the lack of privacy in the ward, so Lillian had his bed placed in the quietest corner of the building, closed in by all the screens they could find, until she managed his transfer to Walter Reed Hospital in Washington. She wanted Frank to have all the time he needed to recover fully, without feeling that the consultancy would sink without him. But his mind was ready before the rest of him, and he grew frustrated sitting in bed in Washington. Shuttling back and forth between Providence and Walter Reed, Lillian kept him abreast of the accounts she handled in his absence. To keep his mind active, she brought him data to be analyzed and drafts of papers to be reviewed. It was another three months before doctors finally thought him well enough to go home.

When Frank returned, he received a hero's welcome. The children were ecstatic to see him, and Lillian had everyone's favorite meals prepared in celebration. It had been six months since Frank saw the children last. The older ones had schoolwork and chore charts to show him, though admittedly they had performed chores less regularly when mom and dad had been gone. Frank could barely recognize baby Fred, who was now walking with the rest of his brothers. Dan, a newborn when his father had left for Oklahoma, was now crawling and getting into things more ably than his father, who still hobbled on a cane. He still walked gingerly, in fact, by the time they set off for Nantucket Beach.

In the months of Frank's illness and recovery, Lillian had fallen into survivalist mode, keeping focused on things that needed her immediate attention and tabling the rest for later. She had lost hair and weight, but she hadn't the luxury of taking days off to rest or be alone. She had run the business, directed caregivers, and instructed children and household staff with directives she had wired home. As the parent in charge, she had decided to do whatever she could to maintain normalcy and calm in Frank's absence. Part of that plan was simply keeping up the pretense of optimism at all times around the children and keeping Frank in Washington until he looked well enough not to worry them upon his return. The other part of the plan was to organize their usual excursion to Nantucket, as if the summer of 1918 were like any other.

As hard as she worked to maintain accounts, the family business had lost significant amounts of money during Frank's convalescence. The losses could not have come at a worse time, for they had just purchased the two old lighthouses in Nantucket that they planned to convert into a summer home and office. The children christened their quirky vacation abode "the Shoe," after the nursery rhyme, not yet aware of how accurate a description it would be. That summer they broke it in by retrofitting it for motion study. Their heights and weights were recorded on the doorjambs, and they adorned the walls with astronomical charts and their parents' management codes for quick reference.

Lillian came to love her summers at the Shoe; the rigorous schedule of the school year grew lax, and the children got the rare opportunity to be carefree kids who made boats and swam off the pier. The young women astronomers who worked at the Maria Mitchell House and Observatory often took the children up to the telescope to look at stars. That summer in 1918, the sea air was just what the doctor ordered to hasten Frank's recovery. Steadily he gained more movement in his limbs and reinstated new chore charts for the children. In the late weeks of summer, he even regained enough vigor to conceive another child with Lillian, a boy who came the following May.

Indeed by the fall, it was as if Frank's near-death experience had never happened. He was back in full force, working for the Pierce Arrow automakers and tending to his local clients. He was off to England for meetings with the Red Cross Institute for the Blind and the Surgeon General's Office. In his absence, he gave Lillian instructions to teach the children the Roth Memory Course, and, when he returned, he and Lillian got to work on laboratory trials for their next book, *Motion Study for the Blinded*. Again, he put Lillian on a rigorous writing schedule, as he thought out loud about developing yet another course for college students—this time strictly in the field of management. Lillian just looked on in amazement. How could he teach others to manage their businesses when he could not stop long enough to manage his health?

Although Frank seemed to put his illness easily out of mind, Lillian felt the weight of the world on her shoulders. Doctors made it clear to her that her husband's heart was severely compromised by the trauma of the spring, and she worried about him obsessively as he returned to his professional engagements. He booked appointments here and presented papers there as if no one had warned him to slow down. Lillian's response was to talk to doctors quietly about what she could do to keep him well. He was likely unaware of the fact that she, too, had charts, ones that monitored his diet and activities. She knew she could not control him, but she had one stipulation to which he could not object: if he insisted on traveling and carrying on at his stressful pace, he was to carry a heart stimulant at all times. By the end of 1918, Lillian had eight children in the house and was pregnant with yet another; she had no intention of raising them without a father. The Great War had officially ended with an armistice in November, followed by the Treaty of Versailles in June. But the war had its lingering effects in the Gilbreth household. It was the great challenge to which Frank had hoped to rise, but which in the end had proven him fallible. Rather than making him legendary, it had turned Lillian's husband into her greatest worry of all.

7

Montclair

An Experiment in Science and Domesticity, 1919–1924[1]

If Frank worried about himself or the family finances, he didn't show it; all hardships were surmountable, he preached, so long as one worked hard and stuck to a plan. Despite the recent setbacks, he thought it wise to purchase a used but well-maintained Pierce Arrow, the car Frank Jr. and Ernestine made famous decades later in *Cheaper by the Dozen*. This was the vehicle the Gilbreths packed into that November of 1919 to embark on another chapter in their harried family life, leaving Providence to live yet again in New Jersey. When they left Plainfield back in 1912, they were a more modest family of seven—parents, grandma, and four living children, with one on the way. Seven years later, the sum of the children more than doubled.

The arrival of baby number ten, John Moller, earlier that spring hastened the move, but the Gilbreths had been contemplating it for some time. The New England Butt Company contract was successfully completed, and it was clear that New York was a more advantageous base of operations, given their clients of late. Frank and Lillian went searching again for a home in the suburbs, but this time they targeted Montclair, a town with reputedly excellent schools that would put them in close proximity to Lillian's aunt Lizzie, on her father's side. They heard it said that Montclair was "an engineers' town." Revisionist efficiency experts

Calvin Rice and Henry Gantt, whom they liked and respected, had long settled in town with their families. This was the commonality with neighbors that had been missing in Plainfield, and Lillian planned to seek out their hospitable wives. Moreover, the town was on the Lackawanna train line, allowing for easy access to meetings and clients in Manhattan. This of all things especially appealed to Lillian, still an intimidated driver of motorcars.

Not every Gilbreth piled into the Pierce Arrow for the road trip to Montclair, despite depictions in *Cheaper by the Dozen*. Mom and Grandma stayed behind, content to follow by train, since Lillian was still nursing baby John and Martha was feeling her years. The women felt comfortable allowing the rest of the children to travel without them, because the oldest girls were becoming competent caregivers in their own right. Ernestine, a preteen, had become little John's special attendant, just as Anne had been Fred and Dan's. With each new baby, an older child adapted their parents' three-point promotional system to home life, learning and mastering skills that she passed down to younger siblings to make the family unit function like a well-oiled machine. In a household that continually expanded, such predictability had its place, though Frank took special delight in disrupting expectations now and again. He seemed utterly amused watching the reactions on his children's faces each time he stopped the car at some dilapidated shack on the way to Montclair and declared it the new Gilbreth residence.

Everyone was relieved when he finally pulled up to 68 Eagle Rock Way, a historic structure set back from the road, nestled in Japanese maples. The boys immediately envisioned making baseball diamonds and football fields of the sprawling side lawns. Martha, meanwhile, quietly took to the flower and vegetable gardens behind the house as Lillian gravitated to the wraparound porch. The barn served as a garage initially, but Frank converted it into a laboratory with a built-in darkroom. He made an office of the large drawing room on the ground floor, with a double desk installed so that he and Lillian could work side by side. Up a flight of stairs, the family slept in six bedrooms; the third floor was reserved for the eldest boy and the rest of the live-in help. By

Thanksgiving the Gilbreths appeared to be comfortably installed and back to their elaborate holiday rituals. Frank and Lillian wasted no time thereafter completing *Motion Study for the Handicapped*, the culmination of research they conducted during the war, before Frank became so suddenly indisposed.

The only one who did not adjust well to the move was Grandma Martha; in her eighty-seventh year, she had grown more withdrawn than Lillian had ever known her to be. When Frank was away, Lillian couldn't help but notice that her mother-in-law was content to rock alone in her chair or nap quietly with the younger children. She cooked less and kept more to herself. Frank sensed what he could not say out loud, that perhaps his mother knew she was facing her final days. He stayed closer to home to spend more time with her, and Lillian quietly stood back, allowing Frank to tend to his mother with final gestures of affection.

When Martha died in 1920, Lillian mourned her deeply. Looking back on her mother-in-law's life, she saw meaning and usefulness. It had essentially spanned the entire existence of the American suffrage movement, from the decade before the Seneca Falls convention to its ultimate victory with the Nineteenth Amendment, and she proved to be the responsible woman citizen for whom suffragists argued that the vote should be a right. No one lived as puritanically free of excess nor raised a son more devoted in return. As a retired teacher and widow, she was impacted by the legislation that first-wave feminists (1848–1920) fought hard for so that women had more control over the assets they brought into their marriages. Martha raised her son on savings feminists fought to let her keep, yet for all her education, competence, and self-sufficiency, she died having never found a political voice of her own. American women won the right to vote officially in August of 1920, and thus Martha's impact on public life, although significant, was indirect—felt largely in her liberation of daughters and a daughter-in-law to make public statements of their own. Once overwhelmed by her headstrong mother-in-law, Lillian had come to appreciate those sacrifices that allowed her to live on her own terms. Rarely have women been lifted on shoulders as square as Martha Bunker's.

But now Lillian wondered how she was going to run the house without her trusted domestic manager to support her. She gave birth to another child on Independence Day that year, a boy named Robert, and she hadn't the discretionary funds to hire housekeepers as she nursed him and ran the business. To afford the new mortgage, Lillian had let go of much of the personnel she had had back in Providence, making her tasks of raising the kids and running the business more daunting than they had ever been. Ever the optimist, Frank assured her that it all could be done, so long as they had a "scientific" plan in place. Their new home, he vowed, would be the site of their most ambitious experiments yet. Their livelihood depended on it.

Of course Frank had been running domestic experiments all along. There was the "buoyancy experiment," for example, which he conducted with Anne when she was just an infant, for he had heard that one could reduce the amount of time it took to teach a child to swim if she had been adapted to water after birth. With a nurse on hand, he submerged the baby in the tub, whereupon she immediately sank and Lillian abruptly terminated the experiment. Swimming was apparently not a task to learn efficiently, but he was determined that his baby girls would walk, talk, read, and learn math more quickly than other kids their age. He also wanted them to become productive participants in an intricate system of chores as soon as possible to turn his household into a machine that essentially ran itself. Upon learning to walk, Anne already took direction from her father about how to remove his slippers from his feet and transfer them to marks drawn on the closet floor; when she came of age, she taught this task to the siblings who followed her. With the birth of each child, Frank improved on his methods and expanded the tasks he expected his children to do. By the time they reached Montclair, many of his domestic processes had been tweaked to perfection.

Frank called his methods perfect because they were utterly scientific—tested and tested again by positivist method. But by definition, modern science was not a domestic affair. Since the rise of professional science in nineteenth-century America, scholars had proclaimed legitimate, disinterested science as research conducted only in the university lab, away from the emotionally charged space of the home. Those who continued to conduct household experiments looked to be amateurs, and yet the Gilbreths collapsed divisions between scientific and domestic, professional and personal space all the same, redefining science in terms that worked for them. They christened the house in Montclair the "Mostulab," short for Motion Study Laboratory; it was the place where they sought refuge from the outside world but also where they experimented with efficient family living.

Back in Providence, the need to remove the tonsils of four of the five eldest children had turned into an opportunity to run experiments in surgical time-saving measures right there in the family parlor. The Remington Typewriter contract, too, provided a chance for the children to be filmed in typing trials in the room where they normally did their homework and practiced their instruments. They served as lab rats for Frank's experiments with color-coded and Braille keys, as Lillian recorded their typos and time trials. But now, with the more spacious accommodation in Montclair, Frank could outfit rooms more completely for motion study. His children now groomed themselves to German lessons simultaneously piped into the walls of the bathroom, and he painted bedroom ceilings with Morse code messages to decipher during morning and nighttime routines. The children grew accustomed to counting in Latin while doing their calisthenics on the baseball diamond, exercising both mind and body at once.

Such measures saved on tutors and hired help and gave the children more experience as managers of processes. They assisted their parents at their clients' plants and stood in for workers in their films, further blurring the line between family and professional experiments. One might have thought them apprentices or junior consultants as they sat around the movie projector in the living room analyzing the movements of women workers packing soap flakes. Before long the older children were whizzes at not only operating the speed clocks and time exposure equipment but also at keeping the family books. They studied the household bills for the hourly services of repairmen and medical professionals to learn the lesson that Time Is Money—one should never let resources go to waste.

From the time the Gilbreth children could walk, talk, and write, they participated in Frank's master plan for the house, one that to outsiders appeared to suppress individuality and micromanage a child's every move. His work charts, for example, regulated the children's daily grooming and chores, and no detail was ignored. Young Martha's chart, for example, listed activities that she was supposed to carry out from the moment she arose in the morning until bedtime, with no minute unaccounted for in between: she was to "hang up wraps" in their designated place; clean her nails; practice her languages, piano, and cello; take her meals; and brush her teeth all at designated times. Her chart accounted for the time it took her to walk to school and organize things needed for the following day; there was no minute to spare for daydreaming or dillydallying, for wasted time could be seen on her chart. When she completed tasks on time, she marked corresponding squares in blue. She marked squares yellow when she did not complete tasks on time, and red if she did not complete them at all. The color coding was a practice Frank adapted from his clients' plants because it allowed him to spot problems and evaluate a worker's progress almost instantaneously.

Girls and boys alike had to do their part to ensure the proper running of the family machine. Thus Frank Jr.'s morning routine also didn't allow for a minute of waste, either: Martha woke him up on the hour, and he was in the bathroom by 7:01. By 7:02 he was playing German records as he brushed his teeth and bathed. He weighed himself and recorded any change on his weight chart at 7:07, combed his hair, washed the ring out of the tub, started the bath for Bill, and wound up the Graphophone at 7:08. By 7:10 he woke Bill and turned on French records to listen to as he dressed. At 7:16 he shined his shoes, and he made his bed two minutes later, straightening his room three minutes after that. If he kept pace, he was down to breakfast at 7:31 on the nose. Any later, and every sibling after him was thrown off of his or her routine.

The children had their "standing order forms," "output charts," "pay charts," "evaluations forms," "telephone charts," "bath charts,"—even charts recording chest expansion at inhalation. The charting seemed obsessive but was part of the Gilbreths' quest to find the "One Best Way" to do all work, including to run a household. A journalist for the *Montclair Times* likened their homestead to a well-run "industrial community," with Frank as the municipal employer, Lillian the manager, and the children their dutiful employees. To prepare his children for the business world, Frank had them submit bids to win contracts for household projects, posting orders for yard work, painting, or repairs, for instance, and then giving the contract to the child proposing the quickest, cheapest services. As if in the factory, each child also had an assigned number for routing intrafamily memoranda, and Lillian constantly reassessed their physical and mental abilities to tailor work to strengths and needs. Rather than assign a single child to dusting throughout the house, for example, she assigned taller children to tabletops and high shelves and shorter children to legs and lower shelves. Heights, weights, and temperaments were regularly reassessed for the purpose of reassignment.

The children bought in to their parents' schemes to some degree, and they took part in their unusual experiments because Mom and Dad instilled the belief that efficiency made them successful people. It was part of the master plan that they skip grades, and most of them did, because they had been taught foreign languages and "mental math" as toddlers. Although such experiments seem dehumanizing, Lillian nevertheless approved because they provided so much insight into the human mind. Watching her children's reaction to the family machine made her sensitive to the psychological needs of workers in the plant, and, in Frank's survivalist worldview, the lessons served the children for the day they finally left home to fend for themselves. As they prepared statements for weekly Family Councils, they learned to get points across succinctly, for Frank timed their presentations and cut them off when they dragged. The Gilbreth children trained and received training from their siblings so that they knew what it felt like to manage others and accept criticism at once. They learned to draft their own charts, choosing wording and paper colors that were precise and psychologically pleasing. Lillian insisted that making a fifteen-year-old file income tax reports was too enriching not to make it mandatory for each child when he came of age. Annie Moller surely would have scoffed at the idea, especially for her granddaughters, and yet the kids had grown so accustomed to their roles that the house had practically come to run itself.

Indeed "efficiency," Frank Jr. recalled, had become "the most over-worked single word in our vocabularies."[2] Each of his siblings chose an outfit the night before to wear the next day—a practice arguably *too* efficient to be practical, until a family research project confirmed that weather forecasts were accurate 85 percent of the time. Sometimes Dad's schemes were fun, but there were times when the Gilbreth kids came to resent all the systematizing, as it was often synonymous with standardization, thrift, and conformity, which made them uncomfortably conspicuous to their peers. Lillian's days of wearing corsets had long ended with her regular birthing of children, and for her daughters she had abandoned silks and expensive embellishments for fabrics that were durable and easily washed. All of it was in the interest of streamlining domestic processes; there was no point, she insisted to them, in wearing coats with buttons not easily washed, easily replaced, or easily handed down to younger siblings. But, as they watched their stylish, more colorful peers out and about, her daughters started to object. Their drab "uniforms" were stigmatizing, they told her. They wanted to buy clothes that accentuated their assets, like other middle-class girls were wearing. Did everything always have to be so practical?

Grandma Moller could rarely intervene from a distance, but she subtly nudged Lillian to soften her stance and let her girls be girls. Having dressed Lillian fashionably as a child, she couldn't help but to send her granddaughters the occasional care package of expensive dresses ornamented with sashes and bows. Lillian graciously accepted them but also reminded Annie that such accoutrements were difficult to keep pressed on her fixed schedule. "Brains are better than clothes," she reminded her mother. In the years that she had been married to Frank, she had grown less and less concerned about how others perceived their eccentric schemes, for they got her through the day when all was said and done. Now she followed Frank's lead, sermonizing about how fashion was fleeting, as were social judgments. Health and happiness were more important in the end.

In future books and lectures, Lillian continued to champion Frank's call for "standardization" in the home. It made sense in a bustling household, she advised, to maintain uniform sets of buttons, kitchen utensils, and underwear, since that made them cheap and easy to replace. But she knew limits that Frank did not, and she bent the rules when they started to cramp a child's sense of self. One casualty for the good of the whole was a price too high to pay for running the household machine. And thus in her home, as in the factory, the *individual* remained her primary interest. She believed in efficiency, but she could also see that, in Frank's haste to write papers and graduate children, something was often lost. When editors looked critically at the manuscripts he dashed off, or when children grew frustrated with Dad's impossible standards, Lillian provided the tact, the art, and the substance to keep life and work running smoothly. She was the astute observer who provided the oil when she saw friction in Frank's many machines. In business, he conceived efficient industrial practices, but she quietly humanized them. At home, she made it her task to improve upon the systems that he installed. As she always said, efficiency was an artful science.

Frank presumed that the children would simply meet the terms laid out in all his schemes, but Lillian knew better than to expect compliance for nothing in return. The key to her children's cooperation was no different than what she espoused in *The Psychology of Management*: incentivize the work and open channels of communication with "management." The children knew that when they truly objected to something, they could voice their concerns to their mother. Of course, there was little her children told her that Lillian did not already know. As the household manager, she studied their faces and body language to gauge their level of "worker satisfaction" and reminded them that they were loved and appreciated for their individual attributes. It was she, not Frank, who changed their routines when they became too tiresome to enjoy. She had learned from her own upbringing in a large family that every child needed to feel special and heard.

As adults, several of the Gilbreth children confirmed that this emphasis on their uniqueness was Mother's alone. Most times, Frank was simply too concerned with a master plan to cultivate or celebrate the individual personalities of his children. He rationalized that the time his children saved could be banked for one-on-one "happiness minutes" to be spent as they desired, but Lillian was often the only parent present to cash them in. "She knew what every one of her individual children wanted, needed, dreaded, and dreamed about," Frank Jr. recalled. "And when a child talked to her, she listened and listened, and made sure she understood." Whereas Dad saw the family as "an all-inclusive group," Mom "saw her children as a dozen individuals, a dozen different personalities, who eventually would have to make their ways separately in the world."[3]

Another partner might have resented having to work so discreetly around her mate's eccentricities, but Lillian knew implicitly that Frank approved of her quiet interventions. In 1920 he penned a poem to his beloved wife of sixteen years—"my absolutely perfect half"—acknowledging her impact on his life and work:

> One thing I'd like to do before I die,
> To place the credit right, for all your work;
> And make the world know that you and not I
> Conceived the steps that found laws where they lurk.
> You were the first to state that all the arts
> And trades and crafts and other things we do
> Could be cut up into transferring parts.
> I'm glad you taught me this until I knew.
> You said that by psychology we could
> Systematize a science that had not
> Been recognized as such by engineers.
> Your work has brought to me the doctor's hood.
> I'm glad you chose me to cast your lot.
> I'm glad to tell the world you have no peer.[4]

Indeed, their joint work was starting to earn Frank the honorary degrees to which the poem alludes, but colleagues were also beginning to acknowledge Lillian for her contributions to the field. In 1921, they awarded her an honorary membership in the Society of Industrial Engineers (SIE), making her the organization's first female honorary member and only the second honorary member overall behind Herbert Hoover. At a ceremony in Milwaukee, Frank beamed with pride and joked that he could no longer hide the truth—his professional success "had come from the sweat of his frau."[5]

There was truth to the wisecrack. Had he known how fruitful their partnership would turn out, he swore that he would have married Lillian immediately, rather than wasting idle months in courtship. Their regular conceiving of children thereafter was, no doubt, the efficiency man's way of making up for lost time. He contended that children could literally be "cheaper by the dozen," and Lillian agreed to test his theory, conceiving a child roughly every year and a half for the next eighteen years. She had been efficient indeed; by 1922 she had birthed twelve children in thirteen pregnancies. Six of her children were boys and six were girls, just as Frank had planned. It is hard to know the extent to which Lillian endorsed this plan or simply reconciled herself to it and embraced it over time. Years later she joked about it in her autobiography:

> Frank had decided, with his usual knowledge of exactly what he wanted, that they would have six boys and six girls. This seemed an easy undertaking to a person who had practically been an only child most of his life, but was a little appalling to the oldest of nine! However, she was all for doing anything he wanted, and he was sure that the same principles of efficiency which worked out on the jobs should make the running of the household and the bringing up of a family easy.[6]

Lillian portrayed her attitude as one of casual acceptance, and indeed it may have been so long after the fact. That she referred to herself and Frank in the third person is yet another indication of her proclivity to dissemble rather than to reveal authentic truths. She undoubtedly hid her private thoughts and feelings as a way of staving off others' judgments and coping with what might otherwise have become an overwhelming existence. Rather than confront her own emotions, she mastered the art of understanding the emotions of others. Perhaps in easing the burdens of workers, she took away lessons that she eventually adapted to her own circumstance.

Jane, the Gilbreths' last child, broke the mold as the one baby born in a New Jersey hospital rather than at home. Until then, birthing had become a predictable routine: Lillian nursed each child from three to nine months before methodically conceiving, carrying, and delivering the next baby in her very own bed. "She'd supervise the household right up until each baby started coming," the older children recalled of her pregnancies. "She had prepared all the menus in advance, and the house ran smoothly by itself during the one day devoted to delivery." Lillian seemed not to mind going right back to work afterward, though admittedly she enjoyed the brief respite of her first meal out of bed. Sitting at the dining room table to Frank's right, no one expected her to serve or pass the food. There was the joy of just sitting back and taking in the sight of all her healthy children.[7]

Lillian's anxiety after Robert's birth subsided with the birth of Jane, since the older girls now more than made up for their grandmother's absence. Anne proved perfectly capable of serving the meals as Lillian tended to infants. The older children took more responsibility for cleaning the house, tending to the younger children, and balancing the family budget when their parents were out of town. The Gilbreths' family system attracted the curiosity of many reporters, who came to Montclair in the early 1920s to witness all this efficiency for themselves. One observed that despite his many rules, Frank still seemed frantic. His wife, meanwhile, reportedly "radiated efficiency" without "the slightest evidence of nervous drive or hurry about her." "There was a calm and placidity—and femininity" that one reporter found "restful and refreshing."[8] The Gilbreth children, too, recognized this special quality in their mother. Although they revered their father, they recognized that it was Mom's humanizing perspective and influence that led to their joint success, both as parents and engineers. Frank once said that his wife's greatest accomplishment was *The Psychology of Management*, but Lillian disagreed. Babies trumped books, she insisted. Almost never, in all her years of streamlining processes at home, did she ever lose sight of the human element.

Frank spent many weeks in 1923 traveling to Germany, England, and the Czech Republic, often to plan sessions for the upcoming International

Congress of Management. As the children got older and more proficient in their chores, he saw no reason why Lillian shouldn't accompany him more regularly on his trips overseas, and he asked her to join him for a seven-week lecture tour in Europe that summer. Lillian had her reservations, but the children encouraged her to go. One of the engagements on the itinerary was not Frank's, but her own—the British Society of Women Engineers had asked her to give its annual keynote address. But Lillian did not make it to England to speak. She became gravely ill just before her departure, and doctors decided that she shouldn't leave her bed, let alone travel. Her health improved only after she underwent an emergency hysterectomy. Her reproductive life had come to an abrupt end.

It is hard to miss the irony in this unfortunate turn of events: for her entire adult life Lillian had defied her mother's fate, proved the exception to this deeply ingrained presumption that a woman's biology was her destiny, the inescapable obstacle keeping her back in public life. For nearly two decades of perpetual pregnancy and nursing, Lillian's physical condition never impeded her, but now, just as she was stepping out on her own professionally, she experienced her first physical limitations.

In all her recollections about this time, Lillian wrote nothing about her feelings. Frank's reaction, too, according to her, was to say little, take stock, and look ahead to the next chapter of their lives. They had had twelve beautiful children, eleven of them still alive and well; their eldest, Anne, was no longer at home, having achieved impressively in high school and gone on to college. Though they still had an infant and toddlers in the house, Frank thought it time to expand their international presence at the World Power Conference in England and then the International Congress of Management in Prague in the summer of 1924. She agreed that the time seemed right to join him in representing the newly established American Management Association (AMA) overseas. As the children grew more and more self-sufficient, the Gilbreths planned to present themselves at meetings as an inseparable pair.

Of course Lillian's motives for accompanying Frank were not merely professional. By attending these events, she could also watch him closely, since he had proved unwilling to monitor himself. Doctors warned her that Frank was still working too much, and several minor bouts with his heart in recent months had put her on edge. In the past, she had sent him overseas with heart stimulants, but it eased her anxiety to know that she would be on hand, heaven forbid, to administer the stimulants herself. Frank knew that his health weighed heavily on her mind, and yet, still, he refused to slow down in the weeks leading up to their European tour. He honored speaking commitments at the University of Michigan, then Harvard, Lehigh, and Columbia. If it was any consolation for Lillian, doctors at the Life Extension Institute told Frank, after one of his consultations, that his heart was holding up well enough to leave town that June. Lillian hung hope on their every word.

Frank was not home for the entire month of May before the trip abroad. His engagements allowed Lillian to spend hours at a time preparing her birthday present to him, a biography of his life, fittingly titled *The Quest of the One Best Way*. On the days Frank spent on the road, she spoke her reminiscences into the Dictaphone and then hired a secretary to transcribe them into a manuscript. Her plan was to present the volume to Frank in London, but there were still so many other things to get done before they left for Europe on the nineteenth of June. Anne was returning from Smith College and transferring to the University of Michigan, and Ernestine was graduating from high school the week before their departure, with a plan to attend Smith in the fall. After the graduation ceremony and all of the accompanying festivities, Frank and Lillian had only days to run errands before embarking overseas.

There were subtle signs that the late nights of travel the month before had finally caught up with Frank. The day after Ernestine's graduation, he slept in, trying to make up for lost sleep on the road. Later than usual, he collected himself to go into town to get visas processed for the impending trip, forgetting to bring the passports he needed with him. He called Lillian from a phone booth at the Lackawanna train station and asked her to look for the passports in his desk drawer. Lillian asked him to hold the line. She found the passports and returned to the phone, but there was silence on the other end. Frank's train must have arrived, she figured, and thought little more about it. But minutes later she heard a knock at the front door. It was a neighbor who had been in town, and he was pale and distraught; a policeman had stopped him and asked him to go to the Gilbreth residence to tell Lillian the shocking news that Frank had dropped dead in the phone booth right there at the train station. According to the doctor who arrived on the scene, Frank did not suffer; his last words were likely the ones he had uttered to his wife before she told him to hold the line.

8

The Widow

Sexism and Breadwinning, 1924–1928

Lillian's survivalist instincts were too acute to mourn openly for her husband. She had bills, babies, and older children who needed to see strength and competence in their mother so as not to fear a world without their father. She sprang into action, much like she had upon hearing that her husband lay dying at Fort Sill during the Great War. With mechanical efficiency she attended to the details of Frank's memorial, having him dressed in his military uniform for a simple service without flowers or music; she knew her husband would have thought them needlessly extravagant. She also knew that Frank wanted his brain donated to Harvard Medical School and thus saw that it was before having his body cremated and his ashes scattered over the Hudson River.

For some time she had feared the worst, but it was no preparation for the tasks of raising the children and running the business alone, fulfilling the responsibilities she and Frank had shared up to that time. Jane, the youngest, was still a baby, and Robert was still a toddler. Naturally Lillian's mother looked at the road ahead of her daughter and grew protective. She offered to take in the children—if not all of them then some of them—until Lillian weathered the immediate storms, but her daughter would not separate her family. Annie Moller could only raise the question she once asked long ago but learned to suppress over the years: Why had her daughter chosen a life of less privilege and more chaos than the one she had known before meeting Frank? Lillian assured her that the life she had chosen was not second rate but the path less traveled, and she felt privileged to have traveled it with a man who didn't insult her by expecting less. "I have over twenty perfect years to remember," she told her mother. "I have had the best . . . he will wait for me." As daunting as the future was, she had no regret about the choices she had made.[1]

For years, Frank had been convening regular Family Councils, for his wife had convinced him that including the children in household deliberations empowered them and promoted independence. Now with Frank gone, Lillian thought the collective input of the children more crucial than ever, and she convened a council to hear how they wanted to proceed as a family unit. Some of them considered the offers of family and friends to take them in, but ultimately they agreed not to be separated. They would use Frank's life insurance payout to keep the whole family together in Montclair, they decided, and they would also help their mother do whatever it took to keep the Gilbreth consultancy afloat. The older siblings immediately got to work on a tighter household budget, selling the Pierce Arrow their father so adored. Martha agreed to be the official keeper of the family books, while her sisters and brothers took turns managing the grocery budget and maintaining the files in the family office.

The older girls contemplated staying home and taking time off from their studies, if only temporarily, until the family finances had been stabilized. This was the one thing that Lillian emphatically discouraged. Her children had been groomed for college, and she insisted that they attend. Anne and Ernestine acquiesced and agreed to leave in the fall, but they also insisted on staying with the family over the summer to help out with their siblings. They would watch them through August so that Mother could leave for London and attend the World Power Conference, just as Dad had planned. By now, they perfected a seamless system: each older child had been assigned one or two younger ones to feed and tutor, and everyone knew their standing orders in terms of chores. The plan that summer was for Anne and Ernestine to take the family to Nantucket, as always. Meanwhile, one of Anne's classmates, Elizabeth Sanders, arranged to be Lillian's traveling companion overseas.

The children worked through the details so carefully that Lillian could only gratefully proceed as planned. She wired the president of SIE asking, in light of recent events, if she could speak at the Power Conference on Frank's behalf, to which she received an unequivocal affirmation of support. Frank's colleagues thought Lillian's participation at the conference a most touching way for a grieving widow to honor her husband. But she did not leave for London clear of conscience. Days before her departure nearly all the children contracted chicken pox, and her youngest four got the measles. If she thought about staying home, her older children convinced her of the unflappability of the domestic system in place. Lillian remarkably left as planned, believing that her departure was what Frank would have wanted.[2]

That she presided over Frank's sessions and gave his papers on the Gilbreth brand of motion study was stunning to her European colleagues. Observers noted that she spoke authoritatively on topics that they presumed had been Frank's preoccupations alone. From England, she went to Holland to tie up ends at the Stork Company, a major client, before heading off to Prague for the International Management Conference. Although she had found it surprisingly easy to deliver papers at the sessions, the tributes to Frank were much harder to endure. The Masaryk Academy held a memorial service in Prague that was, as she described it, a "harrowing experience."[3] She was confronted with eulogies and much of the open mourning that she had managed to escape with her hasty departure from Montclair. Luckily, Elizabeth Sanders proved to be a much-appreciated diversion from the intense show of emotion for Frank; Lillian left Prague hastily to show her young charge the sites of Paris and Berlin, much as Minnie Bunker had showed her when she was the same impressionable age.

After her return to the States, Lillian published favorable impressions of the trip in *American Machinist* and then set forth trying to preserve Frank's legacy in motion studies. In 1925 SIE agreed to publish her biography of Frank, *The Quest of the One Best Way*, in tribute; looking back, she regretted never allowing Frank to see the book when he lived. The only addition she made to the published manuscript was her "final word": "Suddenly, on June 14, 1924, Frank went, not abroad, as he had planned, but 'West,' as soldiers go. The Quest goes on!" This was the extent of her sentimentality in print. As she explained to Cousin Minnie, now she had to proceed with blinders on to fulfill her greatest mission. "The rest is bringing up the children, and proving I deserved all Frank gave me—and that was everything."[4]

After Ernestine, Martha was the next to graduate from high school, but she stayed in Montclair and took "postgraduate" high school courses so that she could assist her mother at home. That summer, the family made the annual trek to Nantucket with Mrs. Cunningham and Tom Grieves. Meanwhile Lillian shuttled back and forth from the island to New Jersey to keep potential irons in the fire. The Society of Electrical Engineers, the Society of Automotive Engineers, the Taylor Society, and the ASME asked her to speak to their members about recent developments in motion study, and Frank's university contacts also invited her to speak at Purdue, Skidmore, and Colgate. For now, it seemed that she would be able to pick up Frank's projects almost exactly where he had left them.

And yet there were clear differences in how she was able to proceed in his absence. Whereas Frank had grown accustomed to first-class accommodations when he was on the road, Lillian booked upper berths on trains and stayed with friends in college towns. Coeducational universities generally paid her $75 a lecture, a rate much lower than Frank's, and women's colleges like Bryn Mawr paid much less. She accepted her payments gratefully, and women collegians often invited her back again and again. Family and friends worried about her, though. If Lillian had been busy before Frank's death, now she truly had not a moment to spare. On the days she was home, she got her kids ready for school, supervised menus and budgets, sewed buttons, wrote the kids at college, read stories, and helped with homework—all in addition to her ten-hour day in the office or the laboratory or meeting with clients.

It is hard to know how well she succeeded in giving everything and everyone their due attention in this trying time. Some of her children insist that, through it all, she rarely missed a class play, a commencement, or a "Be Your Child" day at the Montclair schools, for which she hired cabs to chauffeur her to the elementary, junior high, and high schools for the day. However, any woman who has ever tried to balance work and family knows that no path is chosen without sacrifice, particularly if there is no other breadwinner in the household. Entries in the family log in the months and years after Frank's death indicate large swaths of time when Lillian could not help but be away from home on business-related trips. Her departures became so common that the children made a ritual of waiting for the mailman to arrive with her letters from overseas, much as they once had done for Frank. Upon her return from one of many conferences, Martha met her at the harbor—not to take her home but to drive her to yet another consulting job in Manhattan. From there, she caught a train to an SIE meeting in Washington, ever confident that the older children could tend to daily tasks without her.

As Lillian took over Frank's travel schedule, the intimate knowledge she once gleaned from daily experiences with her children eluded her in ways it hadn't when Frank was alive. For all her talk about the human element, she could no longer deny that she sacrificed it herself from time to time. If one child felt more slighted than the others, it was Jane, the youngest, who barely knew her father and saw her mother infrequently throughout her childhood. Her older siblings thought her spoiled as the youngest Gilbreth, for Mom was not nearly as strict about rules for Jane as she had been for the others. And yet Jane saw it differently, lamenting that she was the only child with no distinctive memories of family vacations with both parents. As she grew into her teens and all of her siblings had left the nest, she got more of her mother's undivided attention, but there were also weeks and months at a time when Lillian worked out of town. Rather than summers in Nantucket, Jane recalled consecutive years of being shuttled off to summer camp so that Mom could go abroad "for the millionth time."[5] An astute observer of human nature, Lillian must have been aware of her daughter's resentments, but there was little she could do as a single mother and breadwinner trying to keep a business afloat.

On the one hand, Lillian's busy schedule suggests that she continued to build upon the momentum Frank had generated for the Gilbreth consultancy. On the other, she travelled far and wide for business that

did not always materialize. Keeping clients was undoubtedly more difficult now that she did it alone. She didn't think it would be, especially
given the honors bestowed on her in recent years. The AMA had offered
her an honorary membership in 1924, much as SIE had three years earlier, and yet this visibility did not bring in paying clients to any significant degree. SIE was more helpful than most societies in that it allowed
women to attend meetings and give papers. Lillian became chair of its
Fatigue Elimination Committee in 1926, which led to her attending the
Fatigue Summer School in Bavena, Italy in 1927. Again in 1929 she enjoyed some acclaim as the only woman in the American delegation attending the World Engineering Congress in Tokyo. And yet, none of
this international activity led to paid contracts closer to home.

As months and years passed since Frank's death, it grew clear that
few engineers on American shop room floors wanted to hire his wife;
their acceptance of her in the past seemed to have been a show of respect
for Frank, not an appreciation for Lillian's distinctive work in the field.
They generally thought that Frank had been the brains of the Gilbreth
operation and Lillian the assistant who typed and kept his files. Apparently, her connection to a prominent husband had been more advantageous than she ever realized—not because her work was unworthy in its
own right but because sexism would have prevented her access to the
opportunities for visibility Frank provided. In widowhood, she now
knew this to be the truth.

Marriage had oddly served as a social cover for Lillian's professional
interactions with prominent male engineers over the years. As her husband's companion, she had been able to interact with Frederick
Winslow Taylor's many disciples and the revisionist efficiency experts
who became both personal friends and associates after the Gilbreths had
moved to Montclair. She attended conferences and annual meetings for
nearly two decades, and men found her a charming conversationalist.
Marriage had freed her to transgress boundaries of gender, but these
boundaries rigidified once she became a widow. Proof of the change
was the extent to which business quickly trailed off after 1924: Within
a year of Frank's death, Lillian had lost her three biggest clients. She
paid visits to Winchester Laundries, Filenes, and other standbys, but
they were reluctant to rely on her for their managerial needs.

Lillian's was a problem of perception that other women faced in the technical fields. Despite being skilled and original thinkers, they watched husbands win acclaim for their joint research, suggesting that marriage could also be an obscuring force when women didn't establish some professional distance from their mates. Even the legendary Marie Curie, perhaps the most famous woman scientist who ever lived, whom Lillian was soon to meet, published alone on occasion to counter the presumption that her husband Pierre Curie was responsible for her innovations. Understanding these dynamics implicitly when he lived, Frank had insisted that his wife publish her dissertation on her own, even if under a gender-neutral name.

Lillian discovered that his protective measures helped little once he was gone, however, much the way Curie discovered that her husband, too, could not protect her from the grave. Lillian, an honorary member of the ASME, was snubbed for regular membership, much as the widow Curie was snubbed by the French Academy of Science. Earlier, men had allowed Kate Gleason, the engineer Lillian had first met in 1905, to become a member of the ASME, but they apparently regretted it, because they were hostile to her ever since. They did not want to make the same mistake with Lillian now that Frank was gone. Like Curie, Lillian appeared to be an interloper in their gentleman's club now that she hadn't a husband at her side.

Lillian decided not to push the issue, for she had to maintain a look of feminine propriety to ensure that she was not stigmatized any further in ways that would hurt her business. It was so much easier to defend one's reputation as a married woman, a truth also confirmed by Curie when French journalists seized on allegations that she, as a widow, had an affair with a married man. With Pierre Curie no longer alive to defend her, male colleagues linked Curie's sexuality and her science, rejecting her as an incompetent scientist and inappropriate woman at once. After 1924, Lillian, too, was in a position to suffer damage to her reputation if she did not tread carefully. To avoid the look of impropriety, she played up her role as mother to a dozen children, staving off criticism that she was mannish in her professional ambitions.

Her strategy worked to some extent, though it might have been more successful had there not been a downside to her maternal image.

As she fulfilled her duties as a mother, she looked appropriately feminine. On the other hand, as a mother, she also looked too sentimental to perform the objective work required in a technical field like engineering. It was immaterial that this stereotyped femininity did not match what men actually observed in her. Such was the paradox that plagued women in science and engineering fields for the rest of the twentieth century.

Despite the fact that American women had just won the right to vote in 1920, their acquisition of political rights did not completely alter prevailing sentiments about feminine passivity or women's traditional place in the home. Increasingly, American women trained for professional work in colleges and universities, but their credentials did not necessarily translate to acceptance in the professional cultures into which they hoped to be integrated afterward. It took Lillian becoming a widow to understand the extent to which engineering's virile image gave it validity and prestige. The engineer conjured in the American mind was rugged and manly; in the industrial sector he was also seemingly blue collar in his affiliations. Although shop floor workers and managers had once felt like Frank was one of them as he rolled up his sleeves and smoked his cigars, they felt differently about his wife.

It was only after Frank's death that Lillian experienced being turned away from a dinner at the University Club in New York, even though she was an invited guest. According to building regulations, women were not allowed on the premises, and now no one made exceptions, even for Lillian. Likewise, when a committee on which she served in an engineering society convened over breakfast at the Engineers Club in New York City, she was turned away once again, and male colleagues did not consider relocating to another venue to accommodate her. When being welcomed as a speaker or guest, colleagues introduced her as Mrs. Frank Gilbreth rather than Dr. Lillian Gilbreth. Frank had always wanted his wife to be "Dr.," but now her PhD did not give her the same title or respect it afforded men.

After a while it was clear that industrial engineers were not interested in hiring Lillian to install the Gilbreth system in their plants, and so she was forced to consider new approaches to earning a living. If she could not get access to shop room floors, perhaps she could teach motion study to managers who could install it themselves. Teaching was, after all, an activity more socially acceptable for women than was hands-on engineering in the 1920s, and to some extent it still is. The role of the pedagogue is one women have long assumed in American life, and few have been better suited for it than Lillian—an observer of teachers, a student of pedagogical theory, and an instructor of her children and industrial managers at the Gilbreth Summer School. The idea to teach first came to her when Robert W. Johnson, vice president of Johnson & Johnson, proposed that she open a school of motion study for his managers. She wouldn't even have to leave home to run it, he assured her; he would send his people to her in Montclair. Lillian had to admit that the idea possibly solved many of her problems. It could provide income while allowing her to perpetuate Frank's legacy in a way that men found acceptable for a woman.

In December of 1924 she placed her first advertisement for the course—a four-month tutorial in the Gilbreth brand of motion study for $1000 per student. Executives from Borden Milk and Barber Asphalt joined the managers from Johnson & Johnson to make the inaugural session more profitable than Lillian could have hoped, though it did not begin auspiciously. Plagued by a virus that tapped her of her usual energy, she was barely able to lift her head when she introduced herself to her students. Her older children encouraged her to keep with the course, but the younger ones interrupted her classes incessantly in those early weeks. The students were exceedingly gracious, pretending not to notice the inevitable distractions with which their instructor coped as a mother working from home. And yet, apparently, her students gleaned much from the course. The next semester, their numbers increased, some even making the trip to Montclair from Germany and Japan. Whereas Frank had advertised relentlessly to build his client base, Lillian conserved her energy, turning students into disciples who propagated her ideas through simple word of mouth. Frank would have been proud of her efficiency. Staying close to home, she had expanded her reach and got her students to introduce the Gilbreth system to engineers on shop room floors as well as in American universities. Motion study was being integrated into college curricula, thus securing Frank's legacy in the field.

Now it was time for Lillian to build a legacy of her own. The field of industrial psychology had gained legitimacy since she had first called for its expansion at the Dartmouth conference a decade earlier. The number of organizations and publications dedicated to the field had grown exponentially, and editors of *Industrial Psychology* and *Iron Age* now asked Lillian to serve as a contributor to its pages. Members of more and more psychology-based organizations asked her to be on their boards or to teach in newly formed institutes dedicated to the discipline. Meanwhile, her motion study course had unexpectedly opened up new avenues of opportunity upon which she wisely seized. Clients were coming to her not only to learn motion study but also to deal with problems they had as businesses that hired women workers and served women customers.

Lillian's reputation as an expert on women industrial workers had grown with her participation in the Woman's Industrial Conference of 1926 and thereafter through her work for the US Department of Labor's Women's Bureau. But it was also the fact that she was a rare woman in management consulting that lent to clients' assumption that she had special insight into women workers and customers, for this was not an expertise many men felt they could claim for themselves. Her school of motion study provided ample opportunity to analyze women's work and consumption firsthand. One of her students, Anne Shaw, had taken her course in the hopes of meeting the needs of women working at the Green Line Sandwich Company; while Eugenia Lies, the head of the planning department at Macy's department store, had left Manhattan to attend Lillian's class in Montclair, convinced that her feminine perspective was what she needed to right her inefficient cashiers and sales staff. Through Lies, Lillian was able to organize field trips for the rest of her students to the cashiering stations of Macy's flagship store. Moreover, she and her daughter Ernestine were allowed to spend an entire month observing employees and customers on the retail floor. Doubling as employees, they got a firsthand look at how workers interacted with customers and operated the cashiering machines.

There was no better time to be gathering her observations. It was the burgeoning age of mass consumer culture, and the relatively wide-ranging prosperity Americans experienced throughout the 1920s led to greater spending on luxury goods. Retailers were eager to make a science of marketing to maximize profits, and women were apparently the key to success. According to retail industry statistics, women consumers were responsible for 85 percent of spending in American households. Executives at the big department stores—Filenes in Boston, Marshall Fields in Chicago, and Macy's in New York—wanted to know the secret to appealing to the woman consumer. They hired sales staffs of attractive, well-dressed women, hoping to portray an image of affluence that female shoppers would want to emulate through spending. Marketing specialists meanwhile honed the art of window dressing to create yet more desire in consumers to spend in their stores. But there was still so much potential for profits in women shoppers that had not yet been tapped. Few of the available business models sufficiently explained the psychology behind women's spending practices, but Lies convinced managers at Macy's that Lillian was qualified to shed light like no other: as both a psychologist and a mother who purchased for the home, she possessed the perfect combination of scientific thinking and artful intuition.

Landing Macy's as a client was quite a coup for Lillian. Frank had tried to win over its managers years before, showing them the flowcharts and reports he had created for Filenes and promising to decrease their labor costs. But he never did secure the contract. That Lillian succeeded speaks to her ability to exploit close relationships with female managers like Lies, but it also speaks to retail managers' growing respect for the field of consumer psychology and their growing appreciation of household consumption as women's special domain. When she was formally hired by the management, Lillian got to work revamping the physical layout of the aisles in the New York store to make it more visually pleasing and easier for its customers to navigate. She achieved her marketing goals quickly, but then management wanted her to motivate its female sales and cashiering staff to make greater profits. How could she make them more productive, managers asked, yet keep them content at the same time?

Lillian left no stone unturned in the New York store, starting by re-organizing the "tube room," where centralized cashiering took place, before moving on to other departments. She created better systems for posting and filing employee records, changed light fixtures to reduce eye fatigue, repadded walls to reduce distracting noise, determined the fewest therbligs for working the cashier desk, and did away with dupli-cate recording on sales checks. She implemented procedures to reduce counting errors and the amount of time customers waited for change. The more efficient operations of the cashiers would have a domino ef-fect, she promised: shorter wait periods would allow clerks to cater to customers more effectively, putting shoppers in a better frame of mind to spend. As the store generated greater profits, female employees would in turn reap rewards in the form of cash bonuses, time off, and promo-tional incentives. Again, Lillian promised a win-win situation.

To assess the skills and proclivities of employees, Lillian used the basic personality tests and scales devised by the National Employee Managers Association, as well as those devised by her friend Donald Laird, who had written *The Psychology of Selecting Men* in 1925. But in-stinctively she doubted the applicability of these scales to the assessment of female workers, and she worried that the data male managers had collected from interviews of female employees was necessarily skewed, given the intrinsic power dynamics involved. She scrapped the data col-lected through conventional means, surmising that if she interviewed women herself, her gender and psychological training would promote greater candor in the interviewees. She had, after all, spent months working the sales floor, establishing trust and camaraderie with the women workers, who perceived her as one of them.

Indeed, once she eliminated the hierarchical relationship between man and woman, interviewer and interviewee, she came up with alto-gether different sets of data than the male researchers had before her. It appeared that problems on the sales floor were largely psychological in origin. Male managers could not motivate their workers in large part because they did not understand the sources of their workers' physical and mental fatigue. Often it had little to do with the physical arduousness of their work, she explained to management, but rather with factors not readily apparent, such as family burdens or social plans after the work shift. To motivate the female workforce, Lillian recommended that managers make concerted efforts to understand the wants and needs of individual employees more thoroughly, both in and out of the store. Toward that end, she revamped practices to open up channels of communication between managers and salesclerks. As she had insisted in *The Psychology of Management*, she promised that the fatigue of individual workers would decrease once jobs were better fitted to their physical and psychological needs. Workers would practically manage themselves once they saw that they had input on the changes being made on their behalf.[6]

Looking back, it appears that Lillian anticipated the human relations approach that was about to emerge in the field of retail management. The historian Laurel Graham calls her "emphasis on individual differences, skills, and satisfactions . . . the intellectual step that had to be taken before management researchers could become cognizant of the power of the group."[7] She showed managers that workers received intangible rewards for their work and that their embeddedness in a social group affected their efficiency and morale ..ore profoundly than had been understood. Appreciating the relationship of the individual to the group was yet another part of mastering the human element, as Lillian saw it. It was an imprecise science, but it was this and an art at once.

Male managers at other stores and organizations soon called on Lillian to unlock the secrets of motivating women to work harder and spend more. The National Retail Dry Goods Association, for instance, paid her to talk to distributors about "What the Customer Wants." Johnson & Johnson, meanwhile, hired her for a project that, until then, no executive had overseen successfully: developing and marketing sanitary napkins. Men with business degrees were stymied about how to amass consumer data on products that women were too embarrassed to talk about in mixed company. Only years before, women had privately made feminine hygiene products themselves, if they used them at all. It had only been since World War I that volunteer war nurses discovered the absorbent qualities of medical gauze and that commercial manufacturers began to create feminine hygiene products with it for purchase in stores. Kimberly Clark began marketing Kotex pads in the 1920s and had won the largest share of the market. But there were still millions of women whom brand managers failed to reach with their hygiene products. Johnson & Johnson set Lillian on the case to find out just what the female consumer wanted and how to market it afterward.

Once again, Lillian's gender was her advantage. She hired a female corps of market researchers to gather data on their target consumers. Her women sent out questionnaires to women in college and conducted face-to-face interviews with young women about menstruation, confident that they would glean more truthfulness than did male researchers in the past. They learned that only 16 percent of respondents were satisfied with products on the market, and 65 percent indicated interest in alternatives. The candid feedback Lillian and her team received from consumers indicated that they wanted greater comfort, protection, and inconspicuousness in a product they could discreetly obtain and throw away. Psychological tests also provided interesting insights on product packaging: in the anomalous case of sanitary napkins, the consumer was not enticed by colorful, fancy boxes; it really was all about how the product performed, its reliance and durability. Responding to what women were telling her, Lillian set out to create a better product. She set up a performance lab in Montclair and started flushing, submerging, and pulling apart hygiene products already on the market to come up with a full-proof design.

It was rare that a corporate bottom line relied on a frank study of women's bodies and attitudes, and Lillian took advantage of the opportunity to amass the most comprehensive study of women's menstrual cycles and body image that had ever been undertaken. Thanks to her, brand managers for Modess napkins were able to come up with a product slogan that was as accurate as it was effective: "Women designed Modess. Johnson and Johnson made it."[8]

Company executives were quick to play up this idea that Lillian had unearthed truths about women that men were unable to discover themselves, much as she supposedly had for the male managers at Macy's and eventually for men at Sears and Roebuck, who hired her to unearth the motivations of its female sales staff in its Philadelphia store. The Dennison Company, too, hired her to perform motion studies of female employees in Boston, Chicago, New York, and Washington, DC. A department store as far away as Belgium came calling in the late 1920s, asking her to develop process charts like the ones she had devised for women workers in the States. Finally, it appeared that Lillian had found a niche of expertise to call her own. It was one that paid the bills and that she likely would have never discovered had she still been married to Frank Gilbreth.

9

Systematizing Women's Operations During the Depression, 1929–1939

The Gilbreth Family Log, which the children kept up sporadically after Frank's death, reveals the new emphasis of Lillian's work in the late 1920s and '30s: Rather than visits to shop room floors, she attended the Homemaker's Conference at Cornell and meetings with home economists at Columbia Teachers' College. She drafted personnel policies for Sears Roebuck, established the Women's Engineering Club of New York City, talked with the First Lady of the United States about Girl Scouting, worked with the Katherine Gibbs Secretarial School, and spoke on "The Reconciliation of Marriage and Profession." Lillian had written on the special needs of women when Frank was alive, since some of their motion studies—from soap flake packing to typing—required an assessment of women's psychological and physiological makeup as workers. But now the study of women's work was practically her bread and butter.

Indeed by 1929 Lillian turned away from the industrial engineers who had turned away from her, and her timing could not have been better. Much of the work she likely would have had with industrial clients— had she been a man—dried up the following decade anyway, as the nation experienced the devastating effects of the Great Depression.

Rather than languish with no work, Lillian re-emerged in the 1930s as an expert for the times, for economic conditions now provided a whole new context for her perspective and skills. She forged new paths in the classroom and department store, and soon she would also innovate the kitchen—a space where frugality, efficiency, and knowledge of women's psychology were in order. For the next decade, Lillian did more than improve women's experience in the paid workplace, she also brought women's domestic operations under the same banners of modernization and efficiency that had lent prestige to men's endeavors. Rather than resist cultural assumptions about her strengths and proclivities, she let them buttress her position of authority in areas where her persona as a mother of twelve and nurturer of the human element was tolerated, if not appreciated and revered. In other words, rather than challenging sexism head on, she turned otherwise demeaned aspects of femininity into assets.

The stock market crash in October of 1929 shook the nation at its cultural foundations. In the decade of depression that ensued, the conventional division of labor between men and women invariably changed, often more completely than Americans' attitudes about it. The work sectors most devastated in these years—farming, steel, and other well-paying, unionized, heavy industries—had long been dominated by male heads of American households. Unemployment in these sectors soared to anywhere between 25 and 33 percent at its worst; by 1933 some thirteen million Americans, mostly men, were out of work, and a significant number of others were woefully underemployed, unable to provide for their families' basic needs. No longer able to make the living they used to, they had lost more than jobs but often their sense of manhood as well. Some men felt so deflated that they left home, leaving women to run households themselves. All told, in the 1930s an estimated 1.5 million men left their families to take to the streets and breadlines. Whether they wanted to or not, more and more women found themselves taking on the double burden of housekeeping and wage earning as a measure of family survival.

Women had already been making their way into paid work the decade before the Depression, but, by decade's end, 26 percent more women occupied positions in the American workplace, totaling almost eleven million overall. Often they entered light industrial work sectors or the pink-collar service trades—clerical work, retail, and food service jobs, for instance—which had been hit less severely than heavy industry. Historically these were occupations toward which female workers had gravitated in greater numbers anyway, as they were often perceived as extensions of women's proper domestic work. More times than not, they were also seasonal, sporadic, part time, and lower paying positions than male breadwinners would generally accept for themselves.

The vast majority of working American women were single before the Depression, but the dire circumstances of families during the 1930s caused married women to mobilize into the workforce like never before. Commentators often blamed them for the rampant unemployment of their husbands, but Lillian knew that the situation was more complicated, that married women workers and unemployed men both had become the victims of exploitative practices taken up in the name of cost cutting and greater efficiency. In her studies on the marriage status of women workers, she confirmed that managers often replaced married women with younger, cheaper workers yet still justified their lower pay as mere "supplemental" to that of male breadwinners. She knew better than anyone that presuming the existence of a male breadwinner in the homes of American women was foolhardy, and yet it rationalized the exploitation and scapegoating of women workers at once. There was a better way, Lillian insisted—much as she had back in the 1910s, when the unions lashed out at Taylor and his scientific managers. Cost cutting need not go hand in hand with cutting jobs or exploiting workers, so long as a sound plan was in place; an emphasis on incentives and conservation was key. She believed that the scientific management of American industry was still the answer to regaining prosperity in the modern age.

Lillian supported employers setting pay scales according to skill rather than gender, but she was careful not to demand living wages for women too vehemently in the national press. Political and labor union activists were lambasted in recent years for their defense of married women workers, for their efforts seemed misplaced in this time of emasculating unemployment for men. A pervasive paradox was still very much alive in American life: despite the necessity of their increased employment outside the home, married women were still supposed to toil and identify as homemakers above all else. Lillian knew this to be true from her own experience of trying to become a breadwinner, but she would have to tread lightly in proposing other ways to view married women's work. Back in 1926 she had introduced the concept of fifty-fifty homemaking—domestic work done by men and women so that more women could pursue careers—and the press had reacted adversely. If the newspaper reports were any measure, Americans were not ready to accept the idea of men comanaging the home, at least not in the years directly before the Depression. If women were working for wages, they were also supposed to take on the double burden of housework without any help from their husbands.

Lillian assured the press that she was not out to create "kitchen husbands" or "kitchen sons." And thus, instead of emphasizing the idea of housework for men, she put effort into infusing prestige into domestic work, lauding the women who mastered it as a profession. Her enlightened brand of feminine domesticity seemed to mitigate the hardships of jobless men in less threatening ways than telling them to make beds and do dishes or emboldening women workers to collectively bargain in the workplace. Manage the double burden of domestic and paid work seamlessly, she told women, and men will see you as sacrificing compatriots, not as competitive foes. It was a Herculean task to ask of women, but it was one that she had long expected of herself.

Lillian's solution to the problems of women workers was subtle and indirect, but it was what more Americans were ready to heed. In essence, she was trying to help working women not by questioning the acceptability of their double burden but rather by giving their domestic work value by making it visible. This idea was not new; in fact, in some ways it was a continuation of efforts begun in the late nineteenth century. The radical feminist intellectual Charlotte Perkins Gilman, most notably, posited the idea of infusing science in the home to lighten women's workload, much as Lillian did twenty years later. But Gilman was more explicit about valuing housework by professionalizing it, that is, by compensating it, so that women could leave it to others as they pursued paying careers outside the home. Like-minded radicals drew up varied blueprints for Gilman's ideas. At the same time Lillian was performing motion studies, for instance, feminists envisioned Gilman's apartment hotel, communal day cares, industrialized laundry facilities, community kitchens, and the like. Little came of them, however. At the turn of the century, American women had prioritized suffrage over the larger economic and cultural revolutions that Gilman sought in the home.

Lillian's ideas found more widespread acceptance than Gilman's in the end, likely because she emphasized domestic innovation for sheer economic necessity, rather than with gender revolution in mind. Indeed, she looked to be helping out American *families* with her innovations, not working women primarily, who seemed to many Americans to threaten traditional family life with their endeavors outside the home. Historically speaking, the most successful efforts to make housework more efficient in America were not carried out in the name of feminism but rather in the spirit of capitalist enterprise and in the effort to lionize the middle-class homemaker. Lillian seized upon this mentality and claimed to be modernizing the American home as a good Progressive would modernize anything else, infusing it with technology and updating women's training for the noble pursuit of homemaking.

In this, Lillian had more in common ideologically with Ellen Swallow Richards, Helen Campbell, and Isabel Bevier, women who had discovered in the late nineteenth and early twentieth centuries that their best prospects for working outside the home lay, ironically, in their ability to work in the name of the home. They were physical scientists trained at major universities who were then refused jobs in their fields. Rather than give up technical work entirely, they jumped through the one window open to them: technical work geared for the home. They reinvented themselves as domestic scientists.

Looking back on their mother's claim to domestic expertise, Ernestine and Frank Jr. could see that Lillian had no choice but to take the same pragmatic approach: "If the only way to enter a man's field was through the kitchen door," they explained, "then that's the way she'd enter."[1] Luckily, by this time, women had already christened the field of "home economics" in academic institutions. University administrators rationalized that, in this period of specialization, modern homemakers needed the advice of experts to run their technological homes. With more access to indoor plumbing, gas lines, and electricity, middle-class homemakers purchased electric irons, vacuum cleaners, gas stoves, washing machines, and iceboxes—items foreign to their mothers and grandmothers. Home economists, many believed, performed a public service as they conveyed new information to help housewives make their homes more efficient and healthful. As they ran time-saving experiments in simulated home settings, they published their findings in journals now dedicated to their quasi-scientific field.

Domestic science had found a place in the university, but increasingly, too, it also found more popular outlets in the years before the Depression. Mary Pattison, author of *The Business of Home Management: The Principles of Domestic Engineering* (1915), oversaw experiments in food preparation, laundry, and family finances from the Federation of Women's Clubs' Household Experiment Station in Colonia, New Jersey, not far from the Gilbreth home in Montclair. Journalists, cookbook writers, and popular advice columnists also fashioned themselves experts of the new technological age. *Ladies Home Journal* editor Christine Frederick cashed in on the idea of experimentation in the home with her popular books on home efficiency. Like Lillian, she took an interest in the psychology of the worker—in this case the woman homemaker. A self-fashioned student of the Gilbreths' motion studies, she found a way to apply their methods to the work of women in the home—and to turn a profit in the process.[2]

Frank and Lillian could have followed Frederick's path, but they didn't. As early as 1912, they had published papers on their systems of reward and incentive for domestic chores, their children serving as their subjects of observation. They had filmed home economists from Columbia Teachers' College performing motion studies of bed making, and Lillian had adopted a cross-sectioned kitchen for the purpose of making yet more motion study films. But Frank was reticent to delve head first into the world of domestic science, nervous that it would compromise his reputation among better-paying industrial clients. Scientific Management was for specialists, they would likely insist, while homemakers were inherently Janes-of-all-trades. Privately, Frank knew better, but it was only after Lillian tried to make it on her own that she revisited her earlier domestic research and reinvented herself as a domestic consultant. Other women were simultaneously making the same transition with great success. The scientist Lucy Maltby, for instance, began developing Pyrex ovenware for Corning Glass Works, finding the business of domesticity more inviting than culturally masculine industries. There was much less resistance, it seemed, when a woman scientist rooted her technical expertise in technologies for the modern home—and, more specifically, for the modern kitchen.

Editors at the *Journal of Home Economics* proved receptive to Lillian's articles on household standardization, as were home economists when she organized a conference on domestic efficiency at Columbia Teacher's College in New York City. Social scientists Elton Mayo and Helen Lynd and many of Lillian's former summer school students attended with over two hundred homemakers and domestic experts, giving the event both prestige and widespread publicity. Before long, Lillian's foray into domestic consulting also became lucrative. In 1927 and 1928, she published *The Home-Maker and Her Job* and *Living with Our Children*, both with the ordinary housewife in mind. From canning baby food to designing workspace, Lillian's books advised on the One Best Way to run a household. Readers were unlikely to have micromotion equipment, so she encouraged them to design homemade experiments. Their children, for example, could reproduce a cyclegraph by retracing mom's movements with a ball of string and pinning it every time she changed direction. Why not make simo charts to establish the best posture for washing dishes, she challenged readers, or count the therbligs to bake a cake? According to her careful count, a homemaker employing her methods could reduce the amount of walking she did while washing dishes from twenty-six miles a year to a manageable nine.[3]

Books and radio addresses spread Lillian's message of home efficiency to a wide audience, but her kitchen designs may have been the most successful of her endeavors. Mary Dillon, President of the Brooklyn Gas Company, asked her to develop a prototypical kitchen for her company's promotional use, the only stipulation being that the kitchen was fitted for gas appliances, since the design was supposed to convince consumers that successful housewifery relied on the use of gas energy. Lillian agreed to Dillon's plan and in 1929 unveiled the

"Kitchen Practical" at the national Women's Exposition, before installing it in its permanent home in the Coney Island sales office of the Brooklyn Gas Company, where housewives walked past it to pay their monthly utility bill.

What women consumers saw before them was a workspace that was circular, rather than linear or parallel—from the refrigerator to the kitchen cabinet, the stove, the sink, and serving table. The diameter of the entire space was no wider than the distance between a homemaker's outstretched arms, and for optimal convenience, the service table had wheels under it so that it could be moved anywhere in the room. Everything in the kitchen could be custom fitted. Demonstrators showed passers-by how the heights of work surfaces could be adjusted to eliminate bending, stretching, and needless fatigue. Whereas male marketers had seen women strictly as a set of uniform consumers, Lillian acknowledged them as renderers of valuable services and as creative individuals. She liked to think that she was "tailoring" their housework to their needs and wants, but also equipping women with information to help themselves.[4]

Other requests to design kitchens followed quickly; for all of them, Lillian found a way to meet the commercial needs of her client while propagating her broader message about practical and fulfilling homemaking. For the Narragansett Light Company, for instance, she fitted a kitchen with electrical outlets to display the company's light fixtures, but she also measured the extremities of the women onlookers at the exhibit site to fit them for appliances that they could adjust to their liking, regardless of whether they purchased anything in the display. She urged women to use her measurements to saw off the legs of tables currently in their kitchens or to put appliances on cinder blocks to minimize on needless bending and stretching when preparing meals. When she exhibited designs for the New York Herald Tribune Institute, a homemaking research facility associated with the Better Homes of America Trade Association, she provided customers with a list of cheaper fixtures and appliances than the ones on display. Indeed her designs encouraged women to be aspirational consumers but industrious ones too. Many walked away from her exhibits with work charts to plan kitchens of their own.

Lillian's kitchens for the Herald Tribune Institute were distinctively smaller than the workspaces architects had designed earlier in the twentieth century. As homemakers grew hard-pressed to afford hired help in the Depression, she catered more to the solitary homemaker who prepared her family's meals herself. Her largest kitchen for the Institute was a mere ten by twelve feet, and she designed even smaller kitchenettes for the "dual-career" couple, which was steadily gaining acceptance, often by necessity. Lillian understood that as the Depression wore on, more married women were taking on the double burden of housewifery and paid work at once, and thus she made kitchens both economical and efficient to suit their needs. One of her designs even served as the wedding gift for her daughter Ernestine, who continued to work as a buyer for Macy's after she got married. No present was more suitable, given the economic times.

Along with kitchens, Lillian also designed items to go into them. There was the "Door Closet," for instance, and the "Management Desk." Both items she touted as quintessentially modern inventions, intended to help the homemaker perform manual and managerial work more efficiently than ever before. The closet was a thin cabinet fastened to the back of the kitchen door that held mops, cleansers, and other items for easy access. The desk, meanwhile, was a streamlined piece of furniture equipped with clock, adding machine, radio, telephone, child reference books, and charts for the organization of domestic chores. Corporate men liked her vision as much as homemakers did, for two years later IBM asked her to develop a similar desk at the Chicago World's Fair to convey the image of two proverbial offices—one in and out of the home.[5] Indeed her Management Desk propagated an image of homemaking that put the homemaker on par with a professional man, creating prestige for it, as well as for the homemaker.

Lillian gave her domestic advice as she took on contracts to train secretaries and reformatory matrons because she saw the relationship between the home and workplace as parallel and reciprocal. She made work at the factory and work in the home seem analogous: If installed correctly, scientific principles could eliminate physical fatigue, the psychological drudgery of manual labor, and low self-esteem in both settings. Lillian reminded women that they had honed the people skills of psychologists and the analytic skills of engineers to run their homes, making them experts as specialized and worthy as any professional man. In this way, she empowered the woman worker in and out of the home.

As the Depression wore on, she also found subtle ways to reintroduce her idea of fifty-fifty homemaking, albeit slightly revised.[6] This was not the splitting of house chores down the middle between men and women, she insisted. It was the delegation of tasks to whoever was in the best position to perform them—man, woman, or child. There was no more denying the fact that more housewives worked a second shift outside the home than ever before and could no longer afford hired help, and thus it made sense that everyone pulled their weight at home. The Depression called for Americans no longer to view housework as emasculating; a new egalitarian outlook about housework was, Lillian gently advised, the key to family survival. Thus her Kitchen Practical adjustments to heights and lengths of workspaces made food preparation easier for women, but stools also brought a child's workspace level to his mother's to make cooking a group effort. In one of the promotional pamphlets for the kitchen, a man in business attire donned an apron and cooked alongside his wife and child with a look of contented bliss.[7] Indeed Lillian wanted to empower the homemaker to embrace domesticity as well as to share its burdens, much as she claimed to have done herself.

Frank would have been impressed with his wife's prolific innovation of products and processes. Just as he had once invented an adjustable scaffold, Lillian designed a foot-pedaled kitchen trashcan to minimize movements. He had once reduced motions for bricklaying, and now she reduced the motions to make the morning coffee. She also developed electric stoves, refrigerators, and washing machines and advised on how to mix a cake, bake it, and clean up the dishes in just a few dozen steps—even if she was not in her own kitchen often enough to follow her own advice. Exhibiters of her Kitchen Practical handed out coffee cake recipes to walkers-by that they claimed to be hers, when they were likely someone else's. Privately her children had referred to one of her culinary experiments as "Dog Vomit on toast," for over the years she had never found reason to learn how to cook.[8] But it did not much matter that Lillian had little time or inclination for homemaking in her own life; her image as mother and technical expert was enough for consumers to think her the ultimate domestic guru.

Indeed this was a woman who wrote *The Home-Maker and Her Job* on a ship traveling across the Atlantic, as she returned from yet another engineering conference overseas. If her readers didn't know her personal circumstances, they recognized that her professional commitments were many, since they were chronicled regularly in the press. It was unlikely that she had time to fold laundry or cook elaborate meals in her model kitchens. She wasn't the homemaker she wrote about, so much as an expert multitasker living life on her rigorous terms. In this there may have been another subtle message in her books and domestic designs. Her kitchens were spaces in which science combined with creativity to turn homemaking into a fulfilling endeavor for the American homemaker. But they were also spaces in which science had the potential to liberate women either confined by physical restraints or cultural presumptions that they should slave all day solely as homemakers. Wheelchair-bound women and sufferers of heart disease benefited from Lillian's motion studies and the specially rigged kitchens she designed for the American Heart Association. But her devices and designs also potentially lessened the time it took to clean and cook meals, freeing women to pursue paid and creative work outside the home.

Frank had instilled in Lillian the importance of marketing, and Lillian had instilled in him the significance of psychological appeals. There was something that undeniably appealed to women about the way Lillian had come to market herself during the trying years of the Depression. If and when she said something subversive, few outwardly detected it. She looked to be that timeless "mother who knows best"— her maternal persona made her trustworthy. For generations, other women had transgressed the boundaries of the home under similar pretenses, first through the Church, and eventually even through government agencies like the National Consumers League and the Children's Bureau, in which women protected workers like a benevolent mother would. Women's moral authority was something presumably acquired through their sheltered existence raising children in the home, and yet it gave them license to speak out and advocate for others in the political arena. In Lillian's case, her benevolent femininity allowed her to write and speak on behalf of women workers who, by virtue of operating outside the home, no longer appeared maternal enough to advocate for themselves.

On the eve of the Great Depression, it also jettisoned her into party politics, for through her domestic engineering projects, Lillian became friend and personal advisor to the most powerful couple in the Republican Party—Herbert and Lou Henry Hoover, who were engineers themselves. When Herbert Hoover had run for President on the Republican ticket in 1928, Lillian backed him enthusiastically, as did Thomas Edison, Henry Ford, and other American innovators who went on to establish the "Engineers' Hoover for President Campaign." A national Committee of Engineers organized to support his candidacy that year, and Lillian took charge of the women's branch of the committee. Male engineers likely thought that her leadership role would be more symbolic than active, but she had other ideas. A savvy public relations strategist, she planned social engagements and photo opportunities for the presidential campaign, including a high-profile breakfast for Lou Henry Hoover at the Waldorf-Astoria. She also scheduled less-publicized meetings with Herbert Hoover to discuss the growing problem of unemployment in technical fields. Industrial engineers addressed the technical aspects of efficiency while turning a blind eye to the human ramifications of their work, she reported. What was required was a more holistic approach, one that mechanized American industry responsibly, met the needs of human workers, and distributed profits more equitably—all while accounting for the consumer's role, too, in recreating national prosperity.

Hoover listened intently, sincerely interested in a woman's point of view. In the eight years since American women had won the vote, few politicians had been savvy in appealing to the female electorate, but Hoover recognized the power to be had through their support. Settlement house pioneer Jane Addams and radical suffragist Alice Paul thought him an ally of women, as did leaders of the National Parent-Teacher Association, the League of Women Voters, and women's college presidents. That Lillian had his ear may partly be the reason that he appeared such a champion of women. She was the maternal figure who best promoted his technocratic vision, couching it in terms that included homemakers. In her essay "Ten Reasons Why I Should Vote for Mr. Hoover," Lillian told women that his faith in science would bring prosperity to the home and consequently bring dignity and prestige to their work as housewives.

After Hoover won the election he called on Lillian regularly. She earned a place in the First Family's inner circle, attending formal dinner parties with dignitaries and casual breakfasts with the First Couple and their dogs on the back porch of the White House. Lou Henry asked her to play an executive role in the National Girl Scouts organization, while her husband beseeched Lillian to accept an appointment to head the women's division of the President's Emergency Committee on Employment (PECE). The decision to accept was not an easy one, even though Lillian and Frank had always committed themselves to civic work. The economy was failing and her children's college tuitions were due. Lillian still had eight children living under her roof and needed more paying contracts to make ends meet. Hoover's appointment would require a redirection of energies and a temporary move to Washington at a time when Lillian was also in mourning. Annie Moller, the Victorian matriarch who had complained incessantly of her weak constitution, passed away at the age of seventy-five, seven years after the death of her professedly heartier husband William Moller.

Once again, Lillian's children proved supportive of their mother's professional plans. The older ones agreed to help Tom Grieves manage household affairs, and the younger children were already accustomed to mother leaving at a moment's notice to tend to clients and to attend events overseas; no doubt they had become more self-sufficient than other children their age. It helped too that Martha, now twenty, was helping to pay the bills with her paychecks from the New York Telephone Company. Still, it was a long time to be away. Lillian left with a heavy heart, taking solace in knowing that at least she was to be joined in Washington by her old college friend Alice Dickson, who agreed to serve as her Assistant Director in the PECE.

It was ironic that she was leaving home just as she was asking American women to step up their roles as vigilant, belt-tightening domestic planners. Her solution yet again during the Depression was to make housework a business, albeit not to question its unpaid status. She doled out advice on how women could perfect the role of domestic manager, spending wisely at home to promote greater employment of men in their local communities. In the interest of enlightened consumption, the PECE distributed information about the hiring practices of American companies, so that homemakers could seek out products and services of those with the best track records for maintaining their workforces. Lillian's "Follow Your Dollar" campaign called on women to buy American goods, but also to take the time to research the manufacturers and retailers from whom they purchased them. "I am here to urge you, the women of the country, to follow your dollar back," Lillian announced over the airwaves in 1931, "I am asking you . . . to check through the stores where you do your own buying to find out what is being done there to stabilize employment and to make work more satisfactory."[9]

Seizing on women's collective power as consumers, Lillian mobilized women's clubs, home economists, and civic organizations to help the PECE collect data on women's spending habits and to publicize how to alter them to improve the economy. Naturally, it was the middle-class woman to whom Lillian specifically appealed, since she had money to spend. "Share the Work," "Give a Job!" and "Spend Wisely," were slogans she publicized in organizations of middle-class women across the country. The PECE's "Spruce Up Your Home" initiative encouraged women with the means to hire out-of-work men to do repairs and improvements on their homes and in their communities. In December of 1930 she published a list of ways housewives could alleviate the hardships of their families and neighbors:

1. Spend wisely, spruce up your house, apartment, clothes, family, and yourself.
2. Spend some money on your house that you planned to save for Christmas shopping.
3. Don't nag or whine even if there is an unemployed person in your family. Nagging, whining women create and prolong areas of depression.
4. Don't use unemployment to decrease wages of your employees.
5. Make sacrifices to protect the children.

6. Give without patronage—accept without humiliation (suffering people are not responsible for the depression).[10]

Her list perpetuated stereotypical ideas about homemakers, since it played up their presumed proclivities to decorate homes and nurture children. But it also imparted the idea that what women did in the private sphere mattered in the public domain. If Americans still believed that women's place was in the home, Lillian showed them that the choices women made there carried social and economic weight.

Under the PECE Women's Division, Lillian set out to open up lines of communication between the government and the average middle-class woman consumer. Where she could, she buttressed her print campaign in women's domestic magazines with local appearances at club meetings or with radio broadcasts that women could listen to directly in their homes. Unlike male bureaucrats, she had an in with the National Council of Catholic Women, the Jewish Welfare Board, the YWCA, and leaders in the General Federation of Women's Clubs, whose members, in turn, distributed her calls to their grassroots organizations to reach millions of women in a short amount of time. Housewives took comfort in this mother of a dozen children sounding so very much like themselves, many of them taking action in their communities as she had urged them to do. Members of women's clubs in Southern California, for instance, hired unemployed office workers to come into their homes to systematize their files and recipe drawers, while Idaho "block mothers" provided social services for families in need.

Herbert Hoover saw in Lillian a woman who resonated on Main Street and could reach out to the female electorate on his behalf. Her ability to convey her message effectively was not surprising, given that she had always been a translator of sorts. For Frank, she had gleaned the human needs of workers and interpreted them to managers. At Macy's she conveyed the needs of the female clerks and cashiers to the men who oversaw their operations. Even at home, she had been the one who understood the needs of individual children to make sure that they were met by the plan for the whole.

Her presumably feminine abilities to observe, sympathize, and communicate looked to be assets through the 1930s, not just to Hoover, but to more and more social commentators who wrote about her in the press. Alongside educator Helen Keller, birth control advocate Margaret Sanger, and the aviator Amelia Earhart, Lillian was chosen by the journalist Ida Tarbell for her list of fifty women who most successfully contributed to the welfare of Americans. *Good Housekeeping* magazine, too, included Lillian on its list of twenty-two nominees for the title of "America's Greatest Living Woman." In 1933 she kept good company with former suffragists and first ladies on the advisory committee of the Congress of Women, soon to be part of the Century of Progress Exhibition in Chicago. Organizers chose her to speak on women's role in advancing human civilization, and her message was the one she had implicitly espoused for decades: The human element—particularly the female element in and outside the home—had to be understood and accounted for. It was the key to prosperity in the modern age.

Finally, Lillian no longer stood in the long shadow cast by her charismatic husband Frank Gilbreth. She paid tribute to him at every public opportunity, but she also created some separation as a means of professional survival, teasing out her ideas from his so that she could establish herself in a solo career. Little did she know that her career without Frank Gilbreth would be far longer than the one she had managed to forge at his side. She had worked as his assistant, his inspiration, and often his better half for twenty years, not knowing that her solo career would thrive for almost fifty.

Afterword

Domesticity on Her Terms

It took her shifting of professional gears in the 1920s and '30s for academic engineers to recognize that Lillian Gilbreth had been innovating the fields of industrial management and psychology all along. Whereas administrators at Berkeley refused her a doctorate degree in 1911, in later decades they named her an Outstanding Alumnus, lauding her for work they once thought undeserving of a degree. Administrators at Rutgers University awarded her an honorary doctorate degree of engineering in 1929, an occasion marking the first time a woman was so honored at that institution. Perhaps it helped that the field of industrial engineering was steadily changing, its practitioners paying more attention to the subjective facets of human psychology that critics once denounced as unscientific and trivial. Because their sensibilities had shifted, Lillian no longer looked to be an outcast so much as a groundbreaking pioneer, an innovator for the modern age.

Lillian received another twenty-two honorary degrees and dozens of awards and engineering society medals, including the coveted Gantt Gold Medal, which Frank also won posthumously in 1945. She accepted these honors graciously, never seeming to resent the ill treatment of her in the past. But the more meaningful gesture to this pragmatic woman was likely the job offer Purdue University President Edward C. Elliott extended her in 1935—a true indication that she had achieved acceptance in institutional science and would be compensated accordingly. For years Lillian had accumulated a swell of admirers on the West

Lafayette campus, where she guest lectured regularly. With the aviator Amelia Earhart, she was eventually hired to serve as a faculty mentor to the few but growing number of female students on campus who were pursuing technical fields.

Other than a visiting professorship at the University of Wisconsin in 1955, Lillian's position at Purdue was the only academic appointment she ever held in her lifetime. For twelve years she received a regular paycheck and sufficient equipment and staffing in her motion studies lab on campus, which allowed her to take on additional consulting work for the Duncan Electric Company and other regional firms. She slept in the student dorms and dined in the cafeteria, interacting with students intimately and often. She and Earhart became mutual admirers and friends, making it all the more devastating when Earhart mysteriously disappeared during her infamous flight over the Pacific Ocean in 1937. Administrators thought it only natural for Lillian to replace Earhart as the official "Consultant on Careers for Women," a position she accepted with a great sense of responsibility, as well as a heavy heart. In time, Lillian also became the first fulltime female faculty member in Purdue's School of Mechanical Engineering. Dividing her energies between motion study and the teaching of home economics and industrial psychology, she had found a balance between old and new methods, solidifying Frank's legacy as she built upon her own in management and domestic science. Lillian once fell prey to rigid boundaries between home life and academic and commercial work; now, in her early sixties, she finally knew what it felt like to move between these realms at will.

If Lillian ever suffered guilt for leaving her children behind in Montclair, the point was moot after 1939. Jane turned seventeen and went off to Sweet Briar College, leaving the Gilbreth "Mostulab" dormant at long last. The trusted handyman Tom Grieves finally retired, and with Lillian rarely home, the house had fallen into a state of disrepair. Rather unsentimentally, she decided to have it demolished and gave away most of her household items. She rented a modest apartment near the center of Montclair, where she could walk to errands or take the commuter train when she was in town. For all the travelling Lillian did in her lifetime, she never mastered the skill of driving a car. Her children worried that now that she lived alone, she would be lonely. Lillian assured them that she wouldn't. Life as a "superannuated bachelor girl" suited her to a tee, she insisted, now that her children were self-sufficient adults. Having grown up in a house with eight siblings and raised a dozen children, the time had come to have a space of her own.

As World War II loomed on the horizon, Lillian looked to be a liberated and modern woman, earning her keep without a man supporting her. Although she lived alone, in a figurative sense, she kept good company. The Depression had already forced more American women than ever to become heads of households and primary breadwinners, and the war soon loosened up gender roles even more, allowing millions to engage in paid work and national affairs. For the first time in history, women could formally participate in the armed forces—not in combat, but in nursing, secretarial, and other supportive roles. Frank had gone to great lengths to don a military uniform, but Lillian's service to country turned out to be more comprehensive than his in the end. President Franklin Delano Roosevelt called on her to devise work simplification plans for crippled and female workers, and in 1944 she teamed up with author Edna Yost to publish *Normal Lives for the Disabled*, a book dedicated to Frank's memory. She sat on the education subcommittee of the War Manpower Commission, on the educational advisory committee of the Office of War Information, and on the women's army and naval auxiliary boards—known commonly as the WACS and WAVES.

Frank and Lillian had anticipated the reorganization of women's industrial work during World War I, but their vision was more fully realized in the world war that followed. Twelve million women worked outside the home at the start of World War II (25% of the total workforce), and 18 million (one-third of the whole) were in the workforce by war's end. Three million of these women occupied positions in war plants, a clear departure from the feminized service trades. Indeed as men vacated better-paying industrial jobs to fight overseas, managers relied on women to rivet along the hulls of battleships and assemble missiles for B-17 bombers. Lillian was among many female engineers who found technical employment in wartime, for firms were in desperate need of their services, as were universities, where faculty members vacated teaching and research positions to fight overseas. Lillian's responsibilities on the Purdue campus only intensified during the war, as they did for many women in technical fields.

Not surprisingly, as millions of American women returned to a life of exclusive homemaking after the war, Lillian was not among them. She continued to teach at Purdue until administrators asked her to retire in 1948, at the still-vibrant age of seventy. She might have mourned the loss of her first regular job had there not been other projects occupying her time. Now she was free to give talks on college campuses and overseas at conferences. Homemakers heard her over the airwaves, and industrial clients called on her to design workspaces and motion studies. She threw herself into volunteer and government work like never before, consulting for the Girl Scouts and serving as one of two women on the Chemical Warfare Board and eventually the Civil Defense Advisory Council under President Harry S. Truman. With no dependents to care for, she devoted more and more of her energy to projects outside the home.

In 1948 she was unexpectedly catapulted further into celebrity. Ernestine and Frank Jr.'s novel *Cheaper by the Dozen* reached bookstore shelves, creating a media storm that forever etched Lillian's image in popular memory—as a devoted mother, rather than as an industrial engineer. Lillian might have been more vocal in her reservations about the book had she not wanted to be utterly supportive of Frank Jr.'s writing career and Ernestine's desire to keep intellectually stimulated, now that she was a fulltime homemaker. But there were facets of the Gilbreths' home life that she didn't think people would understand—particularly the division of labor that she and Frank had worked out to keep their household afloat. In the postwar years psychologists undoubtedly disapproved of their arrangement, recommending instead that women forego careers for exclusive domesticity.

In the final version of their novel, Ernestine and Frank Jr. gave social commentators little to be critical about. Father knew best and Mother knew her limited place in *Cheaper by the Dozen*. Better yet, Mother's work outside the home looked to be virtually non-existent. The dedication read: "To DAD who only reared twelve children and to MOTHER who reared twelve only children," suggesting that Lillian was the doting mother that middle-class women were expected to be in the postwar years. Readers never knew that privately several of the Gilbreth children lamented how little time they had had with their parents in childhood, their father and mother alike. At various junctures Lillian and Frank both worked outside the home, at break-neck pace, overseas, and for long stints of time.

The fictional Lillian embraced her maternity and domestic influence, much as women did in advertisements for toothpaste and soon-to-be popular television shows like *Leave it to Beaver* in the 1950s. But this image was often more prescriptive than descriptive of Lillian and so many American women, who did not live exclusively as "happy housewives." One million women who had not been in the workforce before World War II had stayed in the workforce afterward, albeit typically in underpaid feminized fields. Although the economic prosperity of the 1950s allowed many women to relinquish paid work for domesticity if they wanted to, substantial poverty persisted throughout the United States, and *actual* numbers of women in the paid workforce increased in these years. Even if they wanted to be stay-at-home mothers, many women worked for wages to pay the bills or to maintain the middle-class lifestyle of the iconic happy homemaker. Like Lillian, they essentially flouted the image of contented domesticity at the same time they were keeping up its appearances.

Lillian's kitchens, books, and motion studies, like her image, supported the ideal of happy housewifery as it subtly undermined it. She approved heartily of the technological revolution that occurred in American kitchens in the postwar years, as well as the greater value attributed to homemaking in the 1950s, but she rejected the notion that women should cook and clean better and longer for perfection's sake. Use the latest kitchen appliances if you can afford them, she told homemakers, but only if they will allow you to do housework towards ends of your choosing. There was nothing gained by slaving over tasks that cars, the postal service, or electric gadgets could achieve in half the time using half the human energy.

Of course, any number of medical experts and social scientists disagreed with her theories about the ultimate ends for which domestic technologies should be used. As they allowed for greater efficiency in the home, many feared that they freed up more women to work for a wage, consequently disrupting nuclear family life. Several insisted that female absenteeism in the home was to blame for the increase in social ills—divorce, juvenile delinquency, even breeches in national security. Then again, few of these critics could deny that in Lillian's personal case, her unorthodox combination of paid and domestic work yielded a household of successful and well-adjusted children. There was no evidence of social degeneration in the Gilbreth family, as each child went to a reputable college and earned a college degree.[1] Five of six of Lillian's sons were war heroes, and afterward all of them were gainfully employed professionals and family men. Each of Lillian's living daughters went on to earn a baccalaureate degree, as well as a proverbial "Mrs." degree eventually. Lillian was proud of their accomplishments as mothers and homemakers, though she herself had taken a different path.

In fact, as her daughters settled into domestic life, Lillian traveled like never before. In 1953, at age seventy-five, she went to Europe, Mexico, Hong Kong, and Bengal during the first of three world tours, all to serve clients, attend conferences, and accept awards. Her whirlwind trip to New Zealand, Australia, the Philippines, India, Egypt, Greece, and France, she made remarkably in her still-active eighties. Biographer Jane Lancaster charted her movements in 1964 and noted her attendance at thirty-four conferences that year, just on U.S. soil alone. In the first three and a half weeks of 1965 Lillian gave over twenty lectures, both in the U.S. and in Europe. Her friends and family marveled at the miles she logged and her frenetic pace, which surpassed anything Frank had achieved during the busiest years of his professional life. When the timing worked out, her children and grandchildren saw her during layovers between destinations, but they lamented that she never stayed for very long.

In the 1960s Lillian received honors from the American Institute of Industrial Engineers and the Western Society of Engineers; she became the first honorary member of the Society of Women Engineers, as well as the first woman appointed to the National Academy of Engineering in 1965. The following year civil, electrical, mining, and chemical engineers came together to award her the prestigious Hoover Medal, an indication that she had reached the highest pinnacles of American engineering in the eyes of her professional peers. Her individual acclaim coincided with rumblings of a second-wave feminist movement throughout the United States, one in which women challenged their marginalization in professional fields, technical ones included. In 1964 Lillian spoke to women scientists and engineers about "closing the gap" at an historic symposium at he Massachusetts Institute of Technology. Younger women marveled at how much she accomplished before the Women's Liberation Movement opened doors, and that she had done it without mentoring or road map in hand.

In some ways, it may have helped that she had no blueprints to follow or large shoes to fill, for then she could proceed on terms of her making. She had nothing to lose by rejecting the rules of male scientific managers, and in the end she redefined and expanded them. Sound science, she declared, could be found in the home, in the human element, and in the culturally feminine sphere.

As Lillian advanced into her late eighties, family and friends urged her to consider slowing down. Her itinerary suggests that she was not ready to heed them. She still had clients and meetings overseas that she planned to attend. What she looked forward to most, however, was celebrating Frank's centennial birthday in 1968. She had had a hand in organizing several events to mark the occasion, but invariably she had some health concerns that slowed her down. She did not rest for long, giving talks in England, Ireland, Germany, and on American television shortly afterward. Finally, a personal tragedy grounded her completely. Martha, the daughter who Lillian relied on to keep the family books in her absence, had been diagnosed with cancer and died shortly afterward at the age of fifty-nine. The death of her child seemed to bring on her deterioration more than any of her diagnosed conditions. For nearly fifty-seven years she had lived with the death of her beloved Mary, and now, at nearly ninety years of age, she felt the pangs of yet another daughter gone. It was the blow from which Lillian never recovered.

She moved in with Ernestine and her family in Arizona, becoming, for the first time in her adult life, a dependent of others. She hated that she was someone else's burden, and yet her ailments caused her to require around-the-clock care. When she became too much for Ernestine to handle herself, Lillian's children decided that it was time for Mother to be put in the care of medical professionals at a nearby nursing home.

Ernestine visited her daily, and the others came with grandchildren from time to time. Sadly, the woman who had always been tuned into the thoughts and emotional needs of others was largely unaware of her visitors in the final two years of her life. She died just after New Years Day in 1972, leaving thirty grandchildren and twenty-two great grandchildren behind.

In recent years, historians have tried to give Lillian Gilbreth her due, but it hasn't been easy. So many of her greatest accomplishments occurred in Frank's name and in the private space of the home, hence outside the ambit of most historical record keeping. Fortunately, in her attempt to perpetuate Frank's memory, she managed to hold on to documents that reveal facets of her personal life and individual contributions to engineering. Frank's voluminous "N-file," which she donated to Purdue University, happens to contain publications and correspondence in her hand. After looking through this collection, the historian Laurel Graham estimates that Lillian was responsible for at least 50% of the books and essays the Gilbreths produced, including ones under Frank's name only. "Lillian was more than a popularizer or editor of Frank's ideas," Graham insists, "she was an original thinker whose ideas were just as central to their work."[2]

Lillian Gilbreth coveted the roles of wife and mother, but the truth was that she longed to engage in professional and intellectual pursuits that others believed incompatible with these roles. She made them compatible by becoming a domestic icon, even as she transgressed the traditional image of domestic womanhood. Throughout her life Lillian quietly redefined people's expectations. Although her mother lived a life of invalidism to bear children, Lillian bore babies as she earned degrees and traveled the world. She nursed children and looked over homework as she dictated academic papers. Later she crocheted outfits for grandbabies as she sat waiting to address audiences of professional men. Looking back, her daughter reflected on Lillian's many roles and decided that there was nothing inherently conflicting about them: "To see your own mother able to work all day and then come home and suddenly snap from a 'business man' into a most understanding and sympathetic mother, makes one wish it were possible for more people to do the same."[3]

Lillian Gilbreth never saw womanhood as biological destiny. As she modeled a strenuous life for her children, she proved that one could balance intellectual and family life, home and work, family and career on terms of ones choosing. She raised the status of homemakers by treating them as specialized experts of important work. But she also simplified housework enough to allow women to leave the home to achieve status and economic autonomy through other endeavors. If some of her ideas seemed contradictory, she was proof of their liberating force.

Primary Sources

Gilbreth Management Desk Brochure

A Modern Aid in the Solving of
Home Management Problems

THE new Gilbreth Management Desk might well be called the General Business Headquarters of the Household Manager. Here, in one artistic piece of furniture suitable for kitchen, breakfast-nook, library or sewing room, are grouped all the modern devices necessary to efficient home management.

Built into the upper center is a handsome International Electric Clock which assures constant, accurate time.

Upon opening the paneled doors, we are greeted with a varied and fascinating group of devices, so neatly arranged as to give the appearance of a single unit. In the top compartment a small, distinctive radio is flanked by several books on pertinent household questions. Directly beneath is a typewriter, and below that a specially constructed small-size adding machine for the checking of household accounts and records. In a side compartment, a telephone fits snugly into its place.

Immediately at hand, in compartments at right and left, are located the household money budget and the visible charts containing comprehensive information on food, marketing, cooking, cleaning, health, education, finance and many other important subjects. And, in two neat drawers on either side, we find the cards of a complete household filing system.

THE GILBRE

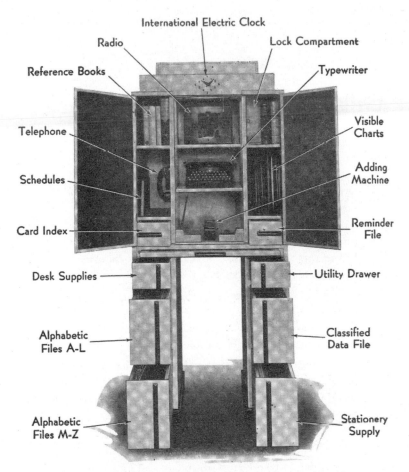

The Gilbreth Management Desk aids in solving household problems
concerning Children, Clothing, Education, Finance and Maintenance,
Food, Health and Medical Care, House Cleaning, Laundry, Recreation and
Culture, Servants, Social Affairs and many other subjects.

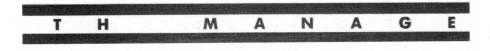

How the
Gilbreth Management Desk
will work for YOU

WHEN is Grandma's birthday?.... I wonder if the taxes are due?..... Goodness, haven't I paid that bill?..... These and many, many other important questions are brought to your attention before they can become embarrassing, by the Management Desk Reminder File.

Perplexing problems regarding the care of the children, the planning of the meals, the arranging of the laundry, and a thousand and one other subjects are all ironed out by the Visible Graphic Charts.

Nor will the grocer, the butcher or the baker ever be paid more than his just due, when all purchase slips and quotations are quickly tabulated on the handy adding machine. What a boon to housekeeping that little device is!

With the Gilbreth Management Desk, the details of your day and week are worked out well in advance. You sail upon a smooth sea, over a well charted course. You save your strength, your money and your peace of mind.

The Gilbreth Management Desk is a beautiful example of the modern trend in furniture design. Made in finishes to harmonize with any interior decoration color scheme.

" ORDER is Heaven's first law," reads an ancient axiom. This artistically designed desk brings home a little nearer Heaven by establishing and maintaining *order* in household planning. The Gilbreth Management Desk will relieve the strain on mind, muscles and pocketbook. It places within easy reach the devices necessary to accomplish specific, routine tasks. Unnecessary steps are eliminated . . . . . unnecessary fatigue is banished.

Lightening the Burden of the Housewife

THE GILBRETH MANAGEMENT DESK

270 Broadway, New York, N. Y.

STUDY QUESTIONS

1. In the primary source document, can you identify how the marketing of Lillian Gilbreth's "Management Desk" encourages American women to be and act? Can this marketing also convey other messages to American women? For whom might the "Management Desk" not be so practical after all?
2. In Chapter 1, young Lillie was raised to adhere to many social rules. Which ones seem to have been abandoned in the American society you know, and which ones linger in various forms?
3. The author pays much attention to details in Lillian Gilbreth's day-to-day home life. Why do you think the author thinks them so significant in telling her story?
4. In Chapter 4, the author questions the extent to which one can call Lillian Gilbreth a "Progressive reformer." What do you think? Would you call Lillian Gilbreth a feminist?
5. In Chapter 9, Lillian Gilbreth addresses the problem of women's work during the Great Depression. How was this problem so different from the problem of men's work in these years? How are these problems still distinct?
6. The author suggests that Lillian Gilbreth redefined "domesticity" through her work and example. Do you agree?
7. If you were to categorize Lillian Gilbreth for the purpose of including her in a history of famous people, what would you call her?

NOTES AND BIBLIOGRAPHY

PREFACE

The two primary archival collections used for this narrative are the Frank and Lillian Gilbreth Collection at Purdue University in West Lafayette, Indiana, and the Lillian Moller Gilbreth Papers in the Sophia Smith Collection of Smith College in Northampton, Massachusetts.

1. Frank Gilbreth Jr. and Ernestine Gilbreth Carey, *Cheaper by the Dozen* (New York: First Perennial Classics, 2002), 205.

2. Such titles were bestowed on Gilbreth, for instance, by *Newsweek* and the state of New Jersey. See Jane Lancaster, *Making Time: Lillian Moller Gilbreth—A Life Beyond "Cheaper by the Dozen"* (Boston: Northeastern University Press, 2004), 332–333.

3. Several works have been more crucial than others in telling Lillian Gilbreth's story and thus are singled out here rather than being repeatedly referred to in the footnotes. First and foremost, Jane Lancaster's *Making Time* has been integral for culling details concerning Gilbreth's personal and professional life. Lillian M. Gilbreth's autobiographical work *As I Remember* (Norcross, GA: Engineering and Management Press, 1998) is the best source on Gilbreth's earlier years, before widowhood, while Laurel Graham's *Managing on Her Own: Dr. Lillian Gilbreth and Women's Work in the Interwar Era* (Norcross, GA: Engineering and Management Press, 1998) is a comprehensive account of Gilbreth's professional life and intellectual contributions to industrial management and psychology. See also Edna Yost, *Frank and Lillian Gilbreth: Partners for Life* (New Brunswick, NJ: Rutgers University Press, 1949); Frank Gilbreth Jr. and Ernestine Gilbreth Carey, *Cheaper by the Dozen* and the sequel *Belles on Their Toes* (New York: First Perennial Classics, 2002, 2003); and Frank Gilbreth Jr., *Time Out for Happiness* (New York: Thomas Y. Crowell, 1970).

CHAPTER 1

1. The best sources for information on Lillian Gilbreth's parents and early years are Lillian M. Gilbreth's autobiography *As I Remember*, 1–61; and Lancaster, *Making Time*, 21–42.

2. Edward Hammond Clarke, *Sex in Education; or A Fair Chance for Girls* (Boston: James R. Osgood, 1873); Sue Zschoche, "Dr. Clarke Revisited: Science, True Womanhood, and Female Collegiate Education," *History of Education Quarterly* (Winter 1989), 545–69; Cynthia Eagle Russett, *Sexual Science: The Victorian Construction of Womanhood* (Cambridge, MA: Harvard University Press, 1989), 116–19.

3. Lillian M. Gilbreth, *As I Remember*, 19–21.

4. William Moller quoted in Lillian M. Gilbreth, *As I Remember*, 66.

CHAPTER 2

1. Many details of this chapter were gleaned from Lillian M. Gilbreth's autobiography, *As I Remember*, 66–75, and Lancaster's *Making Time*, 43–58.

2. William Moller quoted in Lillian M. Gibreth, *As I Remember*, 66.

3. Lillian M. Gilbreth, *The Quest of the One Best Way: A Sketch of the Life of Frank Bunker Gilbreth* (Easton: Hive, 1973), 13–21, originally published by SIE in 1925. "Wife Will Carry on His Work," *The Montclair Times*, June 28, 1924, reel 4, Frank and Lillian Gilbreth Collection at Purdue University, West Lafayette, IN, selected papers (Cleveland, OH: Micro Photo Division, Bell and Howell, 1976). Hereafter cited as GC.

4. Lillian M. Gilbreth, *Living with Our Children* (New York: Norton, 1928), 4–5, 33–34.

CHAPTER 3

1. For details of Lillian Gilbreth's early married life, see Lillian M. Gilbreth, *As I Remember*, 102–13; and Lancaster, *Making Time*, 90–120.

2. "Man's Place Is in the Home," *Philadelphia Public Ledger*, January 31, 1932.

3. Martha Moore Trescott, "Women in the Intellectual Development of Engineering: A Study in Persistence and Systems Thought," in *Women of Science: Righting the Record*, ed. G. Kass-Simon and Patricia Farnes (Bloomington: Indiana University Press, 1990), 147–87.

4. Frank Gilbreth (FG) to Lillian Gilbreth (LG), August 30, 1906; October 1, 1914; November 15, 1914; and August 31, 1914, reel 3, GC.

5. Frank Gilbreth Jr. and Ernestine Gilbreth Carey, *Cheaper by the Dozen*, 205.

CHAPTER 4

1. Mark Twain and Charles Dudley Warner coined this term the "Gilded Age" in their novel *The Gilded Age: A Tale of Today* in 1873. The term was meant to be a social commentary on the post–Civil War years, which coincide with the decades referred to here as the Progressive Age. The term has multiple meanings: "Gilding the lily," a Shakespearean reference, is to adorn needlessly, and indeed Twain and Warner believed the Gilded Age

to be an era of material excess. They also believed that with the advent of new technologies, industries, and the modern corporation, individuals like J. P. Morgan and Andrew Carnegie were amassing wealth in unprecedented amounts to the detriment of the social majority. Thus the era was "gilded" with gold that glittered on the surface but did not extend below the surface. Underneath the thin exterior, in fact, was a much more substantial, baser metal—a larger society suffering great poverty and exploitation.

2. For a discussion of the Gilbreths' eugenicist views, see Lancaster, *Making Time*, 97–99.

3. Lillian M. Gilbreth, *As I Remember*, 115.

4. FG to LG, October 18, 1914, GC.

5. For more on Lillian Gilbreth's intellectual influences, see Graham, *Managing on Her Own*, 56–59.

6. Lillian M. Gilbreth, *The Psychology of Management: The Function of the Mind in Determining, Teaching and Installing Methods of Least Waste* (New York: The Macmillan Company, 1921), 1–3, 18–19, originally published by Sturgis and Walton in 1914.

7. The *Primer* was published in 1912 because Frank Gilbreth had been asked to address "Letters to the Editor" that had been submitted to *American Magazine* in response to Taylor's "Principles of Scientific Management," which the editor printed serially in the March, April, and May editions of the magazine. See Frank Gilbreth, *Primer of Scientific Management* (New York: Van Nostrand, 1912).

8. Yost, *Frank and Lillian*, 193–94; and Lancaster, *Making Time*, 119–20.

9. Frank Gilbreth and Lillian Gilbreth, *Applied Motion Study*, in *The Writings of the Gilbreths*, ed. William R. Spriegel and Clark E. Myers (Homewood, IL: Richard D. Irwin, 1953), 220–31, originally published by Sturgis and Walton in 1917; Sharon Corwin, "Picturing Efficiency: Precisionism, Scientific Management, and the Effacement of Labor," *Representations*, no. 84 (2004): 139–47; and Brian Charles Price, "Frank and Lillian Gilbreth and the Manufacture and Marketing of Motion Study, 1908–1924," *Business and Economic History*, vol. 18, no. 2, (1989): 91.

10. The Gilbreths also referred to themselves as "the good exception" in scientific management. See Lancaster, *Making Time*, 143–51.

CHAPTER 5

1. For Lillian Gilbreth's years in Providence before World War I, see Lillian M. Gilbreth, *As I Remember*, 120–65.

2. Typed reminiscence of Ernestine Gilbreth Carey (1960), Box 3, folder 4, Lillian Moller Gilbreth Papers in Sophia Smith Collection, Smith College, Northampton, MA. Hereafter cited as LMG papers.

3. FG to LG, October 12, 1914, reel 3, GC; Frank Gilbreth Jr., *Time Out for Happiness*, 125; Lancaster, *Making Time*, 127.

4. Lillian M. Gilbreth, *As I Remember*, 129.

5. Mayme Ober Peak, "She Conquers Fatigue—Woman's Greatest Enemy," *Beautiful Womanhood*, February 1923, Box 3, folder 18; "Instruction Card," typed schedule, n.d. (July 11, 1912), Box 4, folder 2, LMG papers; and "Mrs. Gilbreth Gives Formula for Happy Home," reel 4, GC.

6. Peak, "She Conquers Fatigue."

7. Frank Gilbreth's letter about the sight of soldiers in Germany is cited in Lancaster, *Making Time*, 150.

8. FG to LG, October 14, 1914; October 18, 1914.

9. FG to LG, April 5, 1915, reel 3, GC.

10. Lillian M. Gilbreth, "Some Aspects of Eliminating Waste in Teaching" (PhD diss., Brown University, 1915); Lancaster, *Making Time*, 152–57.

11. Lillian M. Gilbreth, *As I Remember*, 139–40.

12. FG to LG, April 29, 1915; May 13, 1915, reel 3, GC.

13. W. H. Faunce to Frank B. Gilbreth, June 6, 1921, reel 3, GC.

CHAPTER 6

1. Lillian M. Gilbreth, *As I Remember*, 147.

2. Lillian M. Gilbreth, *As I Remember*, 148–50.

3. FG to LG, January 7, 1918; January 9, 1918; LG to FG, January 7, 1918; January 8, 1918; [two letters, January, 1918], n. d.; January 18, 1918; and January 31, 1918, reel 3, GC.

4. Lillian M. Gilbreth, *As I Remember*, 157, 151–61.

CHAPTER 7

1. For details on the Gilbreths' systematization of home life, see "Mother's notes on Typewriting-Training," November 24, 1916, Box 3, folder 7; "Daily Schedule of Ernestine Gilbreth" (Martha's schedule included), n.d., Box 3, folder 6, LMG papers; Elizabeth Ellam, "Gilbreth Nantucket Laboratory Most Interesting Place," *Nantucket Inquirer and Mirror*, September 8, 1923; LG to FG, January 25, 29, 1918, reel 3, GC; Lillian Gilbreth, *Living with Our Children*, 173–79; Margaret Ellen Hawley, "The Life of Frank B. Gilbreth and His Contributions to the Science of Management" (master's thesis, University of California, 1925), 113–16, microfilm reel 1, GC; Frank Gilbreth Jr., *Time Out for Happiness*, 17, 129, 132, 147; Frank Gilbreth Jr. and Ernestine Gilbreth Carey, *Cheaper by the Dozen* (New York: First Perennial Classics, 2002), 2, originally published in 1948; Frank Gilbreth Jr. and Ernestine Gilbreth Carey, *Belles on Their Toes* (New York: First Perennial, 2003), 2, 11–12 originally published by T. Y. Crowell in 1950; Lillian Gilbreth, *As I Remember*, 110, 147–69; and Yost, *Frank and Lillian*, 178, 269–70.

2. Frank Gilbreth Jr., *Time Out for Happiness*, 17, 132.

3. Frank Gilbreth Jr., *Time Out for Happiness*, 191; Lillian M. Gilbreth, *The Home-Maker and Her Job* (New York: D. Appleton-Century, 1936), 102, originally published in 1927.

4. Frank's poem quoted in Graham, *Managing on Her Own*, 83.

5. Lillian M. Gilbreth, *Time Out for Happiness*, 170.

6. Lillian M. Gilbreth, *As I Remember*, 107.

7. Lancaster, *Making Time*, 101; Frank Gilbreth Jr., *Time Out for Happiness*, 170; Typed reminiscence of Ernestine Gilbreth Carey, 1960, Box 3, folder 4, LMG papers; Frank Gilbreth Jr. and Ernestine Gilbreth Carey, *Cheaper by the Dozen*, 127.

8. Frank Gilbreth Jr. and Ernestine Gilbreth Carey, *Belles on Their Toes*, 200; Yost, *Frank and Lillian*, 294; Peak, "She Conquers Fatigue"; Ellam, "Gilbreth Nantucket Laboratory Most Interesting Place."

CHAPTER 8

1. LG to Annie Moller, July 6, 1924, Box 11, folder 9, LMG Papers.

2. Hawley, "The Life of Frank B. Gilbreth," 201; and "Family Log," entries from June 14, 1924 to June 22, 1924, Box 3, folder 2, LMG Papers.

3. Lillian M. Gilbreth, *As I Remember*, 195.

4. Lillian M. Gilbreth, *As I Remember*, 194–99; Hawley, "Frank B. Gilbreth," 202; LG to Minnie Bunker, July 6, 1924, Box 7, folder 12, LMG papers; Yost, *Frank and Lillian*, 306; and Graham, *Managing on Her Own*, 86–92.

5. Frank Gilbreth Jr. and Ernestine Gilbreth Carey, *Belles on Their Toes*, 57, 88–89, 131; Gilbreth, *Time Out for Happiness*, 190; "Family Log" entries, 1929–1930; and March 26, 1934.

6. For a comprehensive description and analysis of Lillian Gilbreth's work with the Macy's saleswomen, see Graham, *Managing on Her Own*, 110–41.

7. Graham, *Managing on Her Own*, 141.

8. Yost, *Frank and Lillian*, 321; Graham, *Managing on Her Own*, 218–221.

CHAPTER 9

1. Frank Gilbreth Jr. and Ernestine Gilbreth Carey, *Belles on Their Toes*, 100.

2. Christine Frederick, *The New Housekeeping: Efficiency Studies in Home Management* (Garden City, NY: Doubleday, 1913); and *Household Engineering: Scientific Management in the Home* (Chicago: American School of Home Economics, 1920).

3. Lillian M. Gilbreth, *The Home-Maker and Her Job*; *Living with Our Children*, 21, 92, 96; "Is Your Home a Hazard?" Radio Talk from "America's Little House," February 19, 1935, reel 3, GC; Lillian Gilbreth, Orpha Mae Thomas, and Eleanor Clymer, *Management in the Home: Happier Living Through Saving Time and Energy* (New York: Dodd, Mead, 1955), v.

4. "The Kitchen Practical Designed for the Brooklyn Borough Gas Company by Dr. Lillian M. Gilbreth"; and "Kitchen Practical: The Story of an Experiment."

5. "A Modern Aid in the Solving of Home Management Problems," 1931, Box 14, folder 11, LMG papers.

6. "Man's Place Is in the Home," *Philadelphia Public Ledger*, January 31, 1932.

7. "The Kitchen Practical Designed for the Brooklyn Borough Gas Company by Dr. Lillian M. Gilbreth"; and "Kitchen Practical: The Story of an Experiment."

8. Frank Gilbreth Jr. and Ernestine Gilbreth Carey, *Belles on Their Toes*, 100–103; Graham, *Managing on Her Own*, 182–83.

9. Lillian's radio address, originally an address to the Biennial Convention of Women's Clubs, is quoted from Graham, *Managing on Her Own*, 228.

10. Lillian Gilbreth's list from *The Evening World* printed in Graham, *Managing on Her Own*, 227.

AFTERWORD

1. Anne attended the University of Michigan; Ernestine, Smith; Martha, The Women's College of New Jersey; Frank, Michigan; Bill, Purdue; Lillian, Smith; Fred, Brown; Dan, The University of Pennsylvania; John, Princeton; Bobby, the University of North Carolina; and Jane, Michigan.

2. Graham, *Managing on Her Own*, 11.

3. Martha Gilbreth quoted in Lancaster, *Making Time*, 306.

BIBLIOGRAPHY

Benson, Susan Porter. *Counter Cultures: Saleswomen, Managers, and Customers in American Department Stores, 1890–1940*. Champaign: University of Illinois Press, 1987.

Clarke, Edward Hammond. *Sex in Education; or a Fair Chance for Girls*. Boston: James R. Osgood, 1873.

Corwin, Sharon. "Picturing Efficiency: Precisionism, Scientific Management, and the Effacement of Labor." *Representations*, no. 84 (2004): 139–47.

Des Jardins, Julie. *The Madame Curie Complex: The Hidden History of Women in Science*. New York: Feminist Press, 2010.

Ellam, Elizabeth. "Gilbreth Nantucket Laboratory Most Interesting Place." *Nantucket Inquirer and Mirror*, September 8, 1923.

Frederick, Christine. *Household Engineering: Scientific Management in the Home*. Chicago: American School of Home Economics, 1920.

———. *The New Housekeeping: Efficiency Studies in Home Management*. Garden City, NY: Doubleday, 1913.

Gilbreth, Frank B. *Primer of Scientific Management*. New York: Van Nostrand, 1911.

Gilbreth, Frank, and Lillian M. Gilbreth. *Applied Motion Study*. In *The Writings of the Gilbreths*, edited by William R. Spriegel and Clark E. Myers, 220–31. Homewood, IL: Richard D. Irwin, 1953.

Gilbreth, Frank Jr. *Time Out for Happiness*. New York: Thomas Y. Crowell, 1970.

Gilbreth, Frank Jr., and Ernestine Gilbreth Carey. *Belles on Their Toes*. New York: First Perennial, 2003. Originally published in 1950.

———. *Cheaper by the Dozen*. New York: First Perennial Classics, 2002. Originally published by T. Y. Crowell in 1948.

Gilbreth, Lillian M. *As I Remember: An Autobiography*. Norcross, GA: Engineering and Management Press, 1998.

———. *The Home-Maker and Her Job*. New York: D. Appleton-Century, 1936. Originally published in 1927.

———. *Living with Our Children*. New York: Norton, 1928.

———. *The Psychology of Management: The Function of the Mind in Determining, Teaching and Installing Methods of Least Waste*. New York: Macmillan, 1921. Originally published by Sturgis and Walton in 1914.

———. *The Quest of the One Best Way: A Sketch of the Life of Frank Bunker Gilbreth*. Easton: Hive, 1973. Originally published by the Society of Industrial Engineers in 1925.

———. "Some Aspects of Eliminating Waste in Teaching." PhD diss., Brown University, 1915.

Gilbreth, Lillian M., Orpha Mae Thomas, and Eleanor Clymer. *Management in the Home: Happier Living Through Saving Time and Energy*. New York: Dodd, Mead, 1955.

Graham, Laurel. *Managing on Her Own: Dr. Lillian Gilbreth and Women's Work in the Interwar Era*. Norcross, GA: Engineering and Management Press, 1998.

Hawley, Margaret Ellen. "The Life of Frank B. Gilbreth and His Contributions to the Science of Management." Master's thesis, University of California, 1925.

Heinrich, Thomas, and Bob Batchelor. *Kotex, Kleenex, and Huggies: Kimberly-Clark and the Consumer Revolution in American Business.* Columbus: Ohio University Press, 2004.

Kangiel, Robert. *The One Best Way: Frederick Winslow Taylor and the Enigma of Efficiency.* New York: Viking, 1997.

Lancaster, Jane. *Making Time: Lillian Moller Gilbreth—A Life Beyond "Cheaper by the Dozen."* Boston: Northeastern University Press, 2004.

Levey, Jane. "Imagining the Family in Postwar Popular Culture: The Case of *The Egg and I* and *Cheaper by the Dozen,*" *Journal of Women's History* 13, no. 3 (2001): 125–50.

"Man's Place Is in the Home," *Philadelphia Public Ledger*, January 31, 1932.

Nerad, Maresi. "The Situation of Women at Berkeley Between 1870 and 1915," *Gender Issues* 7, no. 1 (1987), 67–80.

Price, Brian Charles. "One Best Way: Frank and Lillian Gilbreth's Transformation of Scientific Management, 1885–1940." PhD diss., Purdue University, 1987.

———. "Frank and Lillian Gilbreth and the Manufacture and Marketing of Motion Study, 1908–1924," *Business and Economic History*, vol. 18, no. 2, 1989.

Rosenberg, Rosalind. *Beyond Separate Spheres: Intellectual Roots of Modern Feminism.* New Haven: Yale University Press, 1982.

Rossi, Alice. "Barriers to the Career Choice of Engineering, Medicine, or Science." In *Women in the Scientific Professions: The MIT Symposium on American Women in Science and Engineering*, edited by Jacquelyn A. Mattfeld and Carol G. Van Aken. Cambridge, MA: MIT Press, 1965.

Rothbard, Murray N. "War Collectivism in World War I." In *A New History of Leviathan*, edited by Ronald Radosh and Murray N. Rothbard. New York: E. P. Dutton, 1972.

Russett, Cynthia Eagle. *Sexual Science: The Victorian Construction of Womanhood.* Cambridge, MA: Harvard University Press, 1989.

Stage, Sarah, and Virginia B. Vicenti, eds. *Rethinking Home Economics: Women and the History of a Profession.* Ithaca: Cornell University Press, 1997.

Trescott, Martha Moore. "Women in the Intellectual Development of Engineering: A Study in Persistence and Systems Thought." In *Women of Science: Righting the Record*, edited by G. Kass Simon and Patricia Farnes. Bloomington: Indiana University Press, 1990.

Yost, Edna. *Frank and Lillian Gilbreth: Partners for Life.* New Brunswick, NJ: Rutgers University Press, 1949.

Zschoche, Sue. "Dr. Clarke Revisited: Science, True Womanhood, and Female Collegiate Education." *History of Education Quarterly* (Winter 1989): 545–69.

INDEX

Canada, 84
Cancer, 150
Capitalism, 60, 132
Carnegie, Andrew, 61
Cars, 33, 98, 114
Cashiers, 124
Catt, Carrie Chapman, 86
Century of Progress Exhibition in Chicago, 143
Chaperones, 14, 20, 26, 27, 31
Chastity, 27
Chauvinism, 27
Cheaper by the Dozen (Ernestine and F. Gilbreth Jr.), xi, xii, xiii, xiv, 98, 147–148
Chemical Welfare Board, 147
Chicago, 23, 31, 37, 55, 123, 127, 143
    Century of Progress Exhibition in, 143
    University of Chicago, 65
    World's Fair in, 19, 136
Chicken pox, 115
Children, 55, 141, 142
    child labor, 53
    Children's Bureau, 138
    number born to American families, 43–44
Christmas celebrations, 11, 37
Civil Defense Advisory Council, 147
Civil disobedience, 87
Civil War, 17, 18, 53, 90
Clark University, 79
Clarke, Edward Hammond, 6
Clothing, 14, 15, 25, 30, 43, 105
Coal, 17
College education, 6
Columbia University, 26, 27
    Department of Psychology, 28
    Teachers' College, 77, 128, 133, 134
Committee on Industrial Preparedness, 89
Concrete System (F. Gilbreth), 59
Conference on Scientific Management (1911), 65, 66
Congress of Women, 143
Conservation, 68, 85, 130
Consultant on Careers for Women (Purdue University), 145

Cooper, James Fennimore, 19
Corning Glass Works, 134
Corporations, 53
Council of National Defense, 89
Count of Monte Cristo, The (Dumas), 8
Courtship, 14–15, 108
Cunningham (Mrs.), 73, 91, 116
Curie, Marie and Pierre, 119
Cyclegraphs, 68, 134
Czechoslovakia, 109, 115

Dartmouth College, 65, 66, 122
Darwin, Charles, 54, 60
Decision making, xi, 38, 44
Delger, Annie. *See* Moller, Annie
Delger, Frederick, 3
Delger, Lillie, 15–16, 20–21, 25
Dennison Company, 126–127
Dickson, Alice, 140
Dictaphones, 77
Dillon, Mary, 134
Diphtheria, 71, 72
Dishwashing, 134
Division of labor, 129, 130, 147
Divorce, 4, 14, 15, 20, 21, 149
Domesticity, xv, xvi, 9, 10, 12, 13, 20, 24, 26, 27, 43, 44, 73, 77, 86, 105, 129, 136, 147, 148
    sharing domestic work by men and women, 131, 137
Door Closet, 136
Douglas, Helen, 73, 74, 75, 81
Duncan Electric Company, 145

Earhart, Amelia, 143, 145
Earthquake, 47
Edison, Thomas Alva, 18, 49, 139
Efficiency issues, 17, 28, 38, 53, 57, 61, 62, 63, 64, 66, 67, 70, 78, 91, 93, 108, 113, 118, 125
    in the home, 103–105, 129, 132, 133, 134, 148
Electricity, 18, 133
Eliot, George, 9
Elites, 4, 5, 6, 10, 30, 40, 54
Elliott, Edward C., 144

Stock market crash of 1929, 129
Stork Company (Holland), 115
Stratton, George, 50
Strauss, Levi, 3
Suffrage movement, xiv, 86–87, 100, 120, 132
Supreme Court, 53
Surgeons, 84

Tabor Manufacturing Company, 58
Tarbell, Ida, 143
Taylor, Frederick Winslow, 17, 28, 57–58, 61, 66, 72, 118
  death of, 85
  at House Labor Committee hearing, 63, 68, 71
  Taylorism, 58, 62, 67, 68
  Taylor Society, 58, 116
  See also under Gilbreth, Frank Bunker
Teachers, 12, 21, 23, 80, 121
Technological advances, 18, 43, 132, 133, 148
Telephones, 18, 136
Tenement House Act of 1901, 54
"Ten Reasons Why I Should Vote for Mr. Hoover" (L. Gilbreth), 140
Thanksgiving, 11, 100
Theater, 24, 29
Theory of Advertising, The (Scott), 39
Theory of the Leisure Class, The (Veblen), 62
Therbligs, 67, 84, 124, 134
Theta sorority, 24
Thorndike, Edward, 28, 63
Three Musketeers, The (Dumas) 8
Three-point promotion plan, 74, 99
Time Is Money, 102
Time Out for Happiness (F. Gilbreth Jr.), xiv
Time studies, 57
Transcontinental Railroad, 18
Transportation, 18. *See also* Railroads
Triangle Shirtwaist Factory, 62–63
Truman, Harry S., 147
Tuberculosis, 54
Turner, Elsie Lee, 12
Tutoring, 73, 75, 102

Unemployment, 129, 130, 139, 141, 142
Unions, 61–62, 68, 85, 130
United States, 17
  Department of Labor Women's Bureau, 122
  US Postal Service, 18
Urban centers, 17, 43, 53, 54
  rich-poor gap in, 60

Veblen, Thorstein, 62
Victorian age, 2, 5, 12, 18, 43, 55
Vienna, 34–35

WACS/WAVES, 146
Walter Reed Hospital, 95
Walton, Thomas, 71
War Industries Board, 89
War Manpower Commission, 146
Watertown Arsenal, 63
WCTU. *See* Women's Christian Temperance Union
Western Society of Engineers, 149
Wheeler, Benjamin, 23, 25
Wilson, Woodrow, 86, 88, 89
Winchester Laundries, 118
Wisconsin, University of, 145
Women, 62, 63, 66, 70, 77, 96
  in armed forces, 146
  and balance of work and family, 116–117
  as college students/graduates, 22–23, 24, 26, 27, 43, 46
  as consumers, 122, 123, 126, 135, 141, 142
  cultural notions of womanhood, xv, 5–6, 14
  education of, xiii, 21 (*see also* Women: as college students/graduates)
  as empowered, 137
  in engineering, 46 (*see also* Engineering/engineers: female engineers)
  exploitation and scapegoating of, 130
  in factories, 52–53 (*see also* Women: working women)
  female absenteeism in the home, 149